PIRKEI IMAHOT

The Wisdom of Mothers
The Voices of Women

——◆——

RABBI EVE POSEN
LOIS SUSSMAN SHENKER

Foreword by Ruth Messinger

LUMINARE PRESS

WWW.LUMINAREPRESS.COM

Printed in the United States of America

Cover Design by Claire Flint Last

Luminare Press
438 Charnelton St., Suite 101
Eugene, OR 97401
www.luminarepress.com

ISBN: 978-1-944733-15-5
LCCN: 2017932701

In honor of our mothers and daughters

In Appreciation

With gratitude we want to acknowledge the generosity of the following people whose support sustains education and community outreach through the *Pirkei Imahot* Fund.

MAJOR SUPPORT WAS RECEIVED FROM:

Carol Danish from The Danish Family Endowment Fund of OJCF* ❊ Priscilla and Tony Kostiner ❊ Jeanne Newmark from The Newmark Family Fund of OJCF* ❊ Linda and Michael Osherow ❊ Barbara and Stan Rabin from The Stanley and Barbara Rabin Philanthropic Fund of DJCF+ ❊ Diane and David Rosencrantz from The D. Rosencrantz Fund of OJCF* ❊ Fern Winkler Schlesinger ❊ Ardyth Shapiro ❊ Marjorie Pickholtz Spector from the Harry and Marjorie Spector Family Fund of OJCF* ❊ Helen Stern ❊ Carolyn Weinstein from The Women's Endowment Fund of OJCF* ❊ Charlene Zidell from The Charlene Zidell and Daughters Family Fund of OJCF*

ADDITIONAL SUPPORT WAS RECEIVED FROM:

Julie and Tom Diamond from the Julie and Tom Diamond Family Fund of OJCF* ❊ Sara and David Green, Carol and Bob Neuvelt, and David Singer ❊ Sandey and Del Fields ❊ The Given-Back Family Fund of OJCF* ❊ Nicole and Jeff Gullish ❊ Lora and Jim Meyer ❊ The Tarnoff Family Foundation

*The Oregon Jewish Community Foundation
+The Dallas Jewish Community Foundation

Contents

Pirkei Avot

Pirkei Imahot

First Things First

Tzedek, Tzedek Tirdof: Justice, Justice Shall Thou Pursue

ETHICAL BEHAVIOR

TZEDAKAH AND TIKKUN OLAM

MOTHERS' WISDOM

WELL-KNOWN JEWISH WOMEN SPEAK OUT

Foreword

From Ruth Messinger

In my "younger days" of political activism, I was often moved by the folk and labor songs from different eras of the 20th century. One of my favorites, a song composed and sung by Holly Near, has as its title, "There's Something About the Women," and goes on to talk about "the women in my life."

And there is, indeed, something about the women in my life and in our Jewish lives—mothers, rabbis, daughters, scholars, authors, candidates, celebrities, friends, grandmothers—women who have achieved some degree of status or public recognition and women known only to those they raised, sat with in the backyard, or shared their kitchens with.

Wherever they are, these women's perspectives on the world are often different from those of men, reflecting their life experiences—whether raising children or being family caregivers or being mistreated by men or being expected to balance work and family, checkbooks and recipes, dreams and realities for themselves and for others. It is these women and their voices that come alive in these pages in an unusual book that invites you to sit in on and contribute to the discussion.

The men? They have had, throughout history, lots to say. Here's the difference: what they thought and said was captured and written down and then shared generation to generation, often by the women who were not assumed to have thoughts or voices of their own. Sometimes these men elucidated a passage from our sacred texts, often giving it their own spin. Sometimes they disagreed and debated, and—fortunately—our texts include those debates and give us a window into their world views and their differences from each other.

But it was all written down, and it is recited and studied and analyzed today both for what it meant at some earlier point and for what it might be understood to mean or how it might be applied to our same and different situations today.

This book pays tribute to some of these men and some of their teachings, including some of the most famous teachings found in *Pirkei Avot* [Ethics of the Fathers], but it does much more. It captures and elevates the voices and the wisdom of women, recognizing that our experiences and our world views and our perspectives on what matters is different and has too rarely been captured in writing. It gives a place and a printed page for us to have and use for our own purposes.

Not many books are born in a congregation study project, but this one was. It reflects the work of Lois Shenker and her rabbi, Eve Posen, studying *Pirkei Avot* in Jewish dialectical fashion, finding teachings they liked and teachings with which they disagreed, realizing that voices were missing and determining to create them.

They first share with us some of the ancient voices, quoting what we often have heard and may have studied and what we were most likely told were the ethical teachings of our faith. Then they comment on these voices as women living in the 21st century. They bring us their particular perspectives as two women with different life paths and experiences, and they give well-known verses new meaning, disputing some of the texts and adding to others, putting it all into new vessels.

And they invite us in. The book is laid out with questions to the readers, asking for our thinking, our wisdom, our ways to make these verses part of our lives. We are given space—not just physical space on the page but intellectual space and encouragement to reflect on what men have been saying literally for ages.

And then we get to the core of the book, celebrating not only women as commentators on male teachings but women as commentators on their own lives and on ours as well. Women always have had their own views of the world, but too often our voices have been stifled, not deemed worthy of inclusion. In this book, we are given the attention we deserve, a chance to rewrite men's teachings to make them more pertinent to us and, even more centrally, a chance to provide new ideas.

The authors asked many women to share teachings that came from the women in their lives, ideas that they choose to live by and to share with others. Shenker and Posen assumed, correctly, that we women in the Jewish community had our own ideas based on the worlds we know. They created spaces in this book, divided thematically, for women to articulate our own ethical precepts and guides, to share what matters to us, to take what we say in our own circles and put it into the public domain to give new inspiration to others. They are building for women a sense of our own power to be the speakers, teachers, commentators, and leaders for change in the 21st century.

This book is a book of *wisdom for readers* and *wisdom of readers*. As it shares both the ancient text and the more modern commentary with today's women, it asks us questions, pushes us to reflect on what we are reading, gives us opportunities to reflect and challenge, to take what we like, to make our own comments, and to chart our own ways forward. It asks us questions, and it encourages us to write down the answers, to actually enter into dialogue with the writers and editors and, in some ways, with ourselves.

The book is a living text that gives its readers maximum agency to move past differences, to create our own ethical road maps, to reflect, articulate, and then share our wisdom, to actually put down on paper the guidelines by which we do and will live our lives and do our individual parts to help heal the world. It gives us a chance to create our own Torah, our own words of wisdom, our own tradition, our best thoughts to keep us going in hard times.

Ruth Messinger is the Global Ambassador for American Jewish World Service, an international human rights and development organization motivated by Jewish values.

Introduction

✳

Our book, *Pirkei Imahot: The Wisdom Of Mothers, The Voices Of Women*, **was written** to give Jewish women a voice, a voice different from that which had been given them in the past. **It was written** as an opportunity to make that voice newer and stronger within the Jewish world—one that would reflect the 21st century society in which we now live. **It was written** as a result of our own unique experiences as women, mothers, leaders, and teachers in our community, and those of the many women who contributed their own words of wisdom to this book. **It was written** to make a difference!

In reading this book, we believe that you, the reader, will gain wisdom on how to live morally within your community, participate in *tikkun olam* [the repair of the world], and strengthen your ability to make a difference in our world. The questions found throughout the book further provide an opportunity through introspection and self-examination to learn and then apply the lessons found here.

In the summer of 2015, we, Rabbi Eve Posen, the Assistant Rabbi of Congregation Neveh Shalom, and Lois Shenker, a congregant, began a one-on-one study of *Pirkei Avot* [Ethics of the Fathers]. This book is the result of that study.

As we learned together, we discussed what we thought *Pirkei Imahot* would look like. We knew we wanted to reflect on select teachings from *Pirkei Avot*. We knew we wanted our book to include wisdom passed down from mothers to daughters as well as wisdom from Jewish women that together would provide an ethical roadmap in the same way *Pirkei Avot* had provided guidance when it was written. We knew we wanted to include questions designed to help readers ponder and more strongly identify with the ethical teachings, old and new, presented in our book and use these ideas to move forward in their own lives.

The first part of our book, Pirkei Avot, looks at select teachings from the Ethics of the Fathers and reflects upon them from a contemporary woman's point of view. Each is followed by study questions for the reader to consider and a place to record their thoughts and answers.

The second part of the book, Pirkei Imahot, is composed of words of wisdom submitted by Jewish women from across America. They were invited by us to participate on our website, on Facebook, and individually to "join the conversation." They were asked to share their words of wisdom: a favorite saying or quote or teaching that reflected their values, insight they inherited from their mother or other meaningful women in their lives, or their own interpretive words of wisdom from their Jewish heritage, traditions, or Jewish writings. This section is interspersed with study questions as well.

Our vision for this book is to give Jewish women a platform from which to build and strengthen leadership roles and to provide a forum for new and stronger voices within the Jewish world. We hope it will also provide the inspiration, purpose, and motivation to help all of us participate meaningfully in the challenges facing our world today.

Readers will note there is blank space on many pages in this book. That is by design. It is our hope that the reader will make the reading of *Pirkei Imahot* an interactive experience, taking the time to think about, reflect upon, and internalize the contents of our book and take notes or write comments in the space provided.

In *Pirkei Avot* 4:18, we are taught:

"Only with colleagues can your studies be fortified.
Do not rely on your own understanding."

We have lived by this teaching in our study together and recommend this as a possible way for you to approach the questions in this book and other things you choose to study and read.

Things to Know as You Read This Book

There are many available translations for *Pirkei Avot*. The passage excerpts in the first part of *Pirkei Imahot* come from the prayer book *Sim Shalom*. We chose this book because it is the one used by our synagogue for daily prayer and thus accessible to us for our learning. We enjoyed studying this text because of the gender neutral translation the editor uses. For example, the words we have used from *Sim Shalom* for *Pirkei Avot* 2:6, *"Where there are no worthy persons, strive to be a worthy person,"* are correctly translated from the original as *"Where there are no men, strive to be a man."* You will also find that in addition to the translation of the language, the spelling of names may differ in translations as may the number of the chapter or the teaching itself.

In reading the Pirkei Avot portion of our book, the words Mishnah/*mishnah* appear several times. When it appears as Mishnah, with a capital M, it refers to the oral law of our tradition. When it appears as *mishnah*, with a lowercase m, it refers to the individual teaching in each chapter.

Although the words *tzedakah* and *tikkun olam* are found in the glossary, they occur so frequently in this book that we have translated them here. While the literal translation of *tzedakah* is righteousness, its common usage is translated as philanthropy or charity. *Tikkun olam*, translated as repairing the world, reminds us that the act of Creation was incomplete; it is up to humankind to continue to work towards completing it.

PIRKEI AVOT

Introducing Pirkei Avot

irkei Avot, commonly translated as "Ethics of the Fathers," dates back to the Mishnah (the oral law), around 250 C.E. This collection of ethical teachings and sayings of the rabbis reads almost like an ethical will from generation to generation. Within the words and sayings of the six chapters in *Pirkei Avot*, one can gain wisdom on how to act as a leader, teacher, parent, and member of a community—essentially, how to live morally within your community.

What is missing, however, are the voices of women. For instance, in Chapter 1, *mishnah 5*, we read "...do not engage in small talk with your wife." While certainly not meant to be derogatory, the statement is limiting in the scope of the role of women in learning, leadership, and perhaps even family life.

It is with this in mind that we embarked on this journey to read *Pirkei Avot* through our own unique experiences as women, mothers, leaders, and teachers in our community. What follows is our unique voice as women in conversation with the sacred texts of *Pirkei Avot*.

pIRKEI AVOT 1:1

"Moses received Torah from God at Sinai.
He transmitted it to Joshua,
Joshua to the Elders, the Elders to the Prophets,
the Prophets to the members of the Great Assembly.
They formulated three precepts:
Be cautious in rendering a decision,
rear many students,
and build a fence to protect Torah."

MIRIAM RECEIVED THE TRADITION FROM GOD AT SINAI.
She transmitted it to Deborah, Deborah to her daughters.

The chain of our tradition is passed from a mother to her children. Women, for centuries, were the links of tradition, passing on Jewish values and Jewish practices through home life. The world rests on the shoulders of women who have been the source of strength, spirit, and protection of our rituals and their homes. Women have played a central role as teachers throughout our history.

It is this transmission that has sustained our people.

Rabbi Posen

Your Wisdom

pIRKEI AVOT 1:2

"Shimon Ha-Tzadik was one of the last members
of the Great Assembly.
This was a favorite teaching of his:
The world rests on three things—
On Torah, on service of God, and on deeds of love."

THIS IS POSSIBLY ONE OF THE MOST WELL-KNOWN PAS-
sages of *Pirkei Avot*. In it, Shimon Ha-Tzadik implies that, with
these three pillars, the world will be sustained. Torah can be widely
translated as learning. Service of God is our modern day notion of
prayer and upholding the laws of the Torah. "Acts of love" is simple.
Simply loving one another and showing kindness and compassion
to each other will certainly help us to sustain and continue to bring
good and blessing into our world.

But, I read these, and they feel a bit sterile. They don't seem
to hit on what I crave in both my professional life and my life as
a mother.

As a professional, my world rests on the notion of mentorship,
honest conversation, and partnership. When I work in an environment that provides me with these three items I find myself growing,
being sustained, and being uplifted.

As a mother, my world rests on patience, observation, and
deeds of love. These are the three characteristics that I find myself
invoking more than anything else. They are sometimes difficult,
sometimes easy. At times, I need more of one than the other, but
together they help me find balance.

Our world rests on whatever characteristics, actions, or people
we need in order to find our balance and our sanity. *Rabbi Posen*

✳ *Upon what does your world rest?*

Your Wisdom

pIRKEI AVOT 1:4

"Yose ben Yoezer of Tz'redah and Yose ben Yohanan of Jerusalem,
received the tradition from him [Antigonus, of Sokho].
Yose ben Yoezer of Tz'redah taught:
Make your home a regular meeting place for the scholars;
sit eagerly at their feet and thirstily drink their words."

THIS PASSAGE IS CLEARLY REMINDING US THAT OUR
home has a personality. Home is where the heart is, or more
accurately, home is where you make it. I read this text and feel
that my responsibility is to make my home a happy place for my
family and for me and also a place where those whom I love want
to gather. I do this by making a welcome sign for guests coming
over, greeting them with a smile, and sharing toys with little ones.
I do this by welcoming our community into our house for Shabbat
and holidays and by making our "home" the place where we live,
learn, and experience joy and Judaism—whether it is at shul, camp,
or in our actual home.   *Rabbi Posen*

✳ *What is the blessing of your home?*

✳ *How do you achieve that?*

Your Wisdom

pIRKEI AVOT 1:5

"Yose ben Yohanan, of Jerusalem, taught:
...do not engage in small talk with your wife.
Now if this be true for one's wife,
how much more does it apply to the wife of a friend!"

IN TODAY'S WORLD, THIS VIEWPOINT IS UNTHINKABLE! When this passage was written, the Jewish world was a male-dominated society where the highest goal for a Jewish woman was marriage and all that entailed: bearing and raising children, creating and maintaining the home for her family, serving her husband's needs, and basically nothing else.

Today, the role of women has changed significantly. We hold positions in virtually all fields, both secular and Jewish. We are not only capable of far more than small talk—we are capable of engaging the best male minds anywhere in discussion, debate, teaching, and learning. Omitting women in any profession or discourse/dialogue is to lose the keen minds and viewpoints of slightly more than half of the population. Doing so is just no longer acceptable.

Lois

✳ *To what do you think "small talk" refers?*

✳ *How does your definition of "small talk" fit in with this passage as written in ancient times compared to today's world?*

Your Wisdom

pIRKEI AVOT 1:9

"Shimon ben Shetah taught:
Cross examine the witnesses thoroughly,
but be careful in your choice of words
lest something you say lead them to testify falsely."

WHILE THIS *MISHNAH* REFERS TO THE COURTROOM, LIKE many other teachings, it applies to everyday life in other contexts as well, in particular, the impact that words have when used in social media. We should always be careful with our choice of words, in large part because they can never be taken back if we misspeak in the use of them. The childhood phrase, "Sticks and stones may break my bones, but words will never hurt me" is not true. They can hurt, and hurtful words are not easily forgotten. Mindful speech can help us stop using hurtful words and avoid the pain they cause.
Lois

✳ *Are there ways to engage in a difficult conversation without being hurtful?*

✳ *When engaged in a conflict, how can you use your words to lead to more understanding rather than less?*

Your Wisdom

pIRKEI AVOT 1:13

"Hillel taught…
This was a favorite teaching of his:
Knowledge not increased is knowledge decreased."

AS WE AGE, THIS PASSAGE BECOMES MORE AND MORE important. There is a phrase often associated with physical exercise referring to keeping our body fit: "Use it or lose it." I think this applies to our brains and the knowledge we possess as well. Our brains are too valuable to be left to lie fallow. They need to be exercised and lead us to action. In today's world, I think this is particularly true for women. As busy career women or mothers or both, we often do not set aside time to deepen our knowledge. It is both acceptable and essential to find opportunities to strengthen our minds, at any age.

I think one of my greatest intellectual challenges was taking on the study of Hebrew, at the age of 64, with the goal of not only being able to read Hebrew, but to be able to chant Torah as well. When I chanted Torah the first time, it felt like climbing a mountain—one of the single most empowering things I have ever done!

Lois

✳ *What kinds of things could you do to broaden your knowledge?*

✳ *What are the obstacles you face in trying to increase your knowledge?*

Your Wisdom

pIRKEI ΛVOT 1:14

"Hillel taught:
If I am not for me, who will be?
If I am for myself alone, what am I?
And if not now, when?"

THIS WELL-KNOWN TEACHING FROM HILLEL IS TIME-less—its relevance today is still profound. Our opinions about ourselves and other people's opinions about us go hand in hand. In order to take ourselves seriously, we must have self-respect. If we do not value ourselves as individuals and believe in what we think and do, how can we expect others to value us and our actions?

If, on the other hand, we are only for ourselves, what does that say about who we are in terms of our value as human beings. This is what John Dunn meant when he said, *"No man is an island."* We do not function alone in this world. We humans are interdependent one on another, as we should be.

The most important part of this teaching to me is the last line, *"If not now, when?"* We cannot afford to sit back and wait for the right time to act when we see things that need doing, wrongs that need to be made right, lessons that need to be taught. **Now** is the time for action. **Now** is the time to take steps that help to effect change. **Now** is the time to make a difference.   *Lois*

＊ *In what ways are you "for yourself"?*

＊ *In what ways are you "for others"?*

＊ *How would you complete the phrase, "Now is the time to…"?*

Your Wisdom

pIRKEI AVOT 1:15

"Shammai taught:
Make the study of Torah your primary occupation;
Say little, do much... ."

THESE WORDS SPEAK TO ME IN ALL THE ROLES I PLAY IN my life. As women, what we do as role models counts. In both of the lines in this passage, it is in the words "do much" that the most important lesson occurs. It is our moral imperative to take action—to stand up and be counted, to fight for what we believe in.

"Make the study of Torah your primary occupation."

At any age, continuing to study and restudy Torah and Jewish writings helps each of us to stay on higher ground morally and spiritually—to seek new meanings in familiar writings as we, and our situations, change.

"Say little, do much."

This passage is another way of saying "Actions speak louder than words." *Lois*

✴ *Is making "the study of Torah your primary occupation" a realistic goal in today's world?*

✴ *Why or why not?*

✴ *How do you think your actions might have served as a positive or negative role model for others?*

✴ *How have the actions of others served as a positive or negative role model for you?*

Your Wisdom

pIRKEI AVOT 1:17

"Rabban Gamliel taught:
His son, Shimon, taught:
…nothing becomes a person more than silence."

I FIND THIS *MISHNAH* POWERFUL IN THE EXTREME. IT IS often the contrast between sound and silence that not only provides quiet, but time to pause and take stock as well. It is often during the silence, the pause, where clear thinking truly takes place and clarity occurs. It is like giving your brain the chance to take a breath. It is the pause that gives us the opportunity to evaluate and consider before taking action.

I read once that a great pianist was asked why he thought his skill was recognized as being so much greater than other pianists. He answered that it wasn't how he played the notes that made the difference; it was what he did with the pauses and how he used the silence.

Lois

✳ *How do you use silence?*

✳ *Can you think of situations in which keeping silent would help to resolve a problem?*

Your Wisdom

pirkei avot 2:3

"Another teaching of Rabban Gamliel:
Be wary of the authorities!
They do not befriend anyone unless it serves their own needs.
They appear as friend when it is to their advantage,
but do not stand by a person in an hour of need."

THIS *MISHNAH* REMINDS ME OF THE WARNINGS ABOUT choosing your friends wisely or keeping your friends close and your enemies closer. There are friends who you know will be there with you throughout all of life's ups and downs. Those are the people you can call in the middle of the night with an emergency and the ones who will always have your back. But sometimes, we choose wrong, and it only comes to reality when we are bit by envy, greed, or mistrust. Be the friend you want to have. *Rabbi Posen*

✳ *What is the number one quality you look for in an authority figure?*

✳ *What qualities do you look for in a friend?*

Your Wisdom

pIRKEI AVOT 2:5

"Hillel taught:
Do not withdraw from the community.
Do not be sure of yourself till the day of your death;
do not judge your fellows till you stand in their situation.
Do not say 'It is not possible to understand this,'
for ultimately it will be understood.
Do not say 'When I have leisure, I will study,'
for you may never have leisure."

HILLEL SPEAKS OF THE POWER OF A COMMUNITY. IN life, there are moments that might lead us to withdraw into ourselves, like a loss, an illness, or overwhelming news, and that is acceptable for a brief time. But, ultimately, we are meant to be in community, in partnership. We can support one another through ups and downs, reassure one another, and help one another.

Rabbi Posen

✳ *Which of Hillel's rules for life do you think is most important?*

✳ *Why did you choose this rule?*

Your Wisdom

pirkei avot 2:6

"Hillel taught…
This was a favorite teaching of his:
Where there are no worthy persons, strive to be a worthy person."

HAVE YOU EVER HAD THE EXPERIENCE OF BEING IN A GROUP
when the majority opinion or behavior of the group differs with
yours? Not only do you disagree, but you believe the opinion or
behavior expressed is morally, ethically, or practically wrong. This
teaching is telling us to stand up and not concede; it is important
to do the right thing. We have the right, as well as the obligation,
to speak our minds. It is our job to rise above the crowd, to show
others the way—as women, as role models, as human beings.

On a special mission to South Africa in 1988, our group visited
Soweto, a slum outside Johannesburg, which can only be described
as a blight on humanity given its poverty, filth, and inhumane con-
ditions—living in little huts without running water or sanitation
and with raw sewage running through the streets. We were invited
into a small one-room home housing a family, about 14 square
feet. The woman of the household welcomed us to her sparsely
furnished home, which from floor to ceiling was spotlessly clean.
As I looked around the room, this teaching came to mind. She
strove to be a worthy person and found her dignity in the process.
I have never forgotten it.   *Lois*

* *What does the word "worthy" mean to you?*

* *In what ways might you "strive to be a worthy person"?*

* *Is speaking up or acting on an issue always worth the
   fallout that may come from it?*

* *What other options are there?*

Your Wisdom

pirkei avot 2:8

"Another favorite teaching of his [Hillel]:
More flesh, more worms; more possessions, more worries;
more wives, more witchcraft; more maidservants, more thievery.
However—
more Torah, more life;
more study with colleagues, more wisdom;
more counsel, more understanding;
more good deeds, more peace.
The acquisition of a good reputation brings personal gain,
but one who has acquired Torah has acquired eternal life."

THIS TEXT SEEMS TO IMPLY THAT THERE IS A GIVE AND take with the good and bad we encounter in our world. *"More wives, more witchcraft; more maidservants, more thievery"* on the surface might appear to be offensive to us living in our egalitarian and politically-correct world. When the *Mishnah* was written, it was simply implying that the more of something good you have, the more you worry about the impact it will have on your life.

Torah here stands in for learning. A person who can learn from anyone, young or old, lives on forever because of the ability to listen with an open mind and heart. Some of the best lessons I've learned have come from the preschool children I've worked with. Personal development comes when we open our ears and hearts to learning from one another and to listening to each other.

Rabbi Posen

✳ *How do you believe we gain a "good reputation"?*

Your Wisdom

pirkei avot 2:15

"Rabbi Eliezer taught:
...repent one day before your death."

THIS PASSAGE IS TRICKY. IT IS SUPPOSED TO BE. SINCE none of us knows the exact moment of our death, how can we repent one day before it? The message in this teaching is a reminder to live each day *as if* it were our last, with a clean slate. By repenting each day, our behavior and actions are the better for it and so are we. Following this teaching on a daily basis can raise us to a higher standard and challenge us to keep on our toes. This passage tells us to repent now, not to wait for "someday."   *Lois*

✳ *How can you make this teaching a part of your daily routine?*

✳ *Is just saying "I am sorry" enough for repentance?*

✳ *What other things might you do to achieve repentance?*

Your Wisdom

PIRKEI AVOT 2:18

"Rabbi Shimon taught:
Be careful when you recite the Sh'ma and the Amidah.
When reciting the Amidah do not make your prayer
a prescribed routine but a plea for mercy and grace before God;
as it is said: 'For God is gracious and merciful,
patient and abounding in love, taking pity on evildoers.'
Do not regard yourself as an evil person."

THE OPENING STATEMENTS IN THIS TEACHING ARE A plea for mindful prayer rather than routine prayer.

While this passage suggests a plea for mercy and grace in our prayers, it does not mention gratitude.

I am particularly struck by the last sentence: "Do not regard yourself as an evil person." This is a concept I wholeheartedly endorse, because I believe that the power of positive thinking makes a difference!

Even when we make a mistake or do something wrong, we should not think of ourselves as being evil. How much better it is to think of ourselves as being human, with the capacity to make a mistake, to forgive others, and to forgive ourselves as well. I think this is an especially important concept to teach children. Rather than say to a child, "You are a naughty child," how much better to say, "You made a mistake. This was not a good thing to do, but we all make mistakes, and they can be corrected." These words carry with them the additional blessing of being able to ask forgiveness, remedy the situation, and, even more importantly, the possibility of changing our behavior for the future. *Lois*

✳ *What does "mindful prayer" mean to you?*

＊ *Do you agree or disagree that gratitude should be a part of prayer?*

＊ *Why or why not?*

Your Wisdom

PIRKEI AVOT 2:19

"Rabbi Elazar taught:
Be diligent in the study of Torah;
be armed with knowledge to refute a heretic;
be aware for whom you labor,
and that your Employer can be relied upon to reward your labors."

I READ THIS PASSAGE AND WONDER WHAT IT MEANS TO be "armed with knowledge." We hear all the time that the pen is mightier than the sword. Thus, our words are certainly weight-bearing and important, but how can we use them as a weapon? We can tear someone down by berating them or build them up with encouragement. We can also use knowledge as a means of spreading love. Knowledge is power. *Rabbi Posen*

✳ *With what knowledge are you equipped?*

Your Wisdom

PIRKEI AVOT 2:20

"Rabbi Tarfon taught:
The day is short, the task is great,
the workers indolent, the reward bountiful,
and the Master insistent!"

IF EVER THERE WAS A TEXT ABOUT PARENTING, THIS IS it! It feels as though there is never enough time; there is so much to do; and don't get me started on the terrible twos-fours! And yet, we do it. We do it because it is what is important; we become parents because the bountiful rewards beat out anything else we might expect. We do it because of the moments of sweet, unexpected kisses; we do it because of those moments that take our breath away. Rabbi Tarfon reminds us that a job to do must be done, even with challenges along the way.   *Rabbi Posen*

✳ *What is the BEST part of parenting?*

Your Wisdom

pIRKEI AVOT 2:21

"Rabbi Tarfon taught…
This was a favorite teaching of his:
You are not obliged to complete the task,
neither are you free to desist from it."

THIS MAY WELL BE MY VERY FAVORITE TEACHING FROM *Pirkei Avot.* It has been a guiding principle for me as an individual, a mother, and a teacher. I love the fact that it is a moral imperative, clearly stated in its importance on the one hand, while on the other hand giving us permission to complete a task on our own timeline. I think of it as being given a free pass by adding three invisible words, "at this time," to the first line.

Given all the problems we see in today's world and the sheer size and scope of them, not having to complete the task is singularly important as well. It would be impossible to complete the task of making the many changes our world needs to be a just place for all people, but there are steps we can take to work towards that end. Small steps count.   *Lois*

✳ **As an individual: How do you think having an out has aided you in making the choice to move towards completion of a task?**

✳ **As a mother: How could you use this passage to teach your child about having a conscience?**

✳ **Do you think the "escape clause" makes a difference in this teaching?**

✳ **As a teacher: What kind of message does this give your students?**

Your Wisdom

pirkei avot 3:2

"Rabbi Hananiah, the Deputy High Priest, taught:
Pray for the welfare of the Government,
for if people did not revere it,
they would swallow each other alive."

TODAY, MANY AMERICANS ARE PRAYING DAILY FOR THE welfare of our government. This is not because of a concern for not revering our government. Rather, it is our fear for its safety and its future. The rabbis who wrote this passage understood the value of law and government. We who live in a democratic society understand its value even more.

We have to remember that living in a democratic society is a privilege, one for which we not only have to be appreciative, but also one in which we have to participate. *Lois*

✳ **What can we, as citizens, do to revere/protect our government?**

✳ **How can we insure its future?**

Your Wisdom

pIRKEI AVOT 3:14

"Rabbi Dosa ben Harcinas taught:
Morning sleep, midday wine, children's prattle,
loafing in the meeting places of the ignoramus—
all of these will ruin a person's life [literally take a person out of the
world]."

RABBI DOSA BEN HARCINAS CLEARLY NEVER HAD SMALL
children! The sweet sound of a child engaging in the world, peo-
ple-watching, sleeping in occasionally, and certainly sharing a
"l'chaim" with friends might take you out of the world of business,
politics, or work, but they certainly can put you into the world
around you. Like everything, this teaching is about moderation.

Rabbi Posen

✳ *What activities, on the surface, might seem like a waste*
of time but actually add tremendous value to your life?

Your Wisdom

pirkei avot 3:15

"Rabbi Elazar Ha-Modai taught:
A person who profanes the sacred,
despises the Festivals,
shames others publicly,
annuls the covenant of our father Abraham [circumcision],
and contemptuously perverts the meaning of Torah—
though steeped in learning and the performance of good deeds—
shall have no share in the world to come."

INTENTION MATTERS. IF YOU ARE DOING THE RIGHT thing for the wrong reason, you may as well not do it at all. You cannot pick and choose the good you want to do in the world. We should always strive to be kind-hearted, well-intentioned, and true to our core beliefs. Speaking out of both sides of your mouth will get you nowhere. This teaching reminds us that we must act with integrity, with truth, and with purpose when we engage in the world around us. *Rabbi Posen*

✳ *How do you teach others to be true to their whole selves?*

Your Wisdom

pIRKEI AVOT 3:16

"Rabbi Yishmael taught:
Be compliant with your seniors, be affable with your juniors,
and greet every person with a cheerful manner."

AS A SENIOR, I CAN ATTEST TO THE FACT THAT SENIORS like to be taken seriously—having others listen to our concerns or opinions becomes increasingly important. And, having folks be compliant with us is one less thing we have to deal with as we age.

By the same token, juniors are often not taken seriously and often their opinions are not either. Being affable and respecting their ideas is a gift to them.

Just as important, we need to be sure our seniors have the skills to take care of themselves or are taken care of when needed. We also need to be sure our juniors are given the skills and preparation to do so when it is their turn. It is our job as mothers and daughters to be sure this happens.

Finally, greeting every person with a cheerful manner sets the tone for future dealings with this person. Others see you as agreeable as well as cheerful, and you have made someone feel good in the process. It's a win-win situation.   *Lois*

✳ ***How can you demonstrate these qualities to the seniors and juniors in your life?***

Your Wisdom

pIRKEI ΛVOT 3:21

"Rabbi Elazar ben Azariah taught:
No Torah, no worldly occupation; no worldly occupation, no Torah;
no wisdom, no piety; no piety, no wisdom;
no knowledge, no understanding; no understanding, no knowledge;
no sustenance, no Torah; no Torah, no sustenance."

ANOTHER WIDELY KNOWN PASSAGE OF *PIRKEI AVOT*,
this teaching reminds us that there is a give and take in our relationships. It is all about finding the balance between how much is
too much or too little to survive. A modern version of this *mishnah*
might add something about "no technology, no connection; no
connection, no technology" in that we often strive to find the balance between connecting digitally and connecting in person with
those around us. What is important to keep in mind is the need
to strive towards balance and basic understanding of our needs,
wants, desires, and wishes.
Rabbi Posen

✳ *What dichotomy speaks the loudest to you?*

Your Wisdom

pirkei avot 4:1

"Ben Zoma taught:
Who is wise? Those who learn from everyone... .
Who is mighty? Those who conquer their evil impulse... .
Who is rich? Those who are content with their portion... .
Who is honored? Those who honor all people."

THESE WORDS ARE AS TRUE TODAY AS THEY WERE WHEN originally written. May we strive to embody them in our lives—as women, mothers, role models to others.

Enough said! *"All the rest is commentary."*   *Lois*

✳ *In your experience, who is wise?*

✳ *In your experience, who is mighty?*

✳ *In your experience, who is rich?*

✳ *In your experience, who is honored?*

Your Wisdom

pIRKEI AVOT 4:2

"Ben Azzai taught:
Pursue even a minor mitzvah [commandment] and flee from an
aveirah [transgression]:
for one mitzvah generates another and one aveirah generates another,
and the penalty for an aveirah is another aveirah."

THIS IS THE EQUIVALENT OF "WHAT GOES AROUND, comes around." Doing good deeds is infectious, and evil works the same way. It is our job to help and serve others, model goodness and kindness, and act with generosity so that we can create the chain reaction of positive impact. We are intricately connected through our deeds. As parents, it is our job to model the behavior we hope to see in our future. As teachers, it is our job to teach the good we wish to see.

Rabbi Posen

✳ *What can you do to pay it forward?*

Your Wisdom

pIRKEI AVOT 4:3

"Ben Azzai taught…
This was a favorite teaching of his:
Do not disdain any person;
do not underrate the importance of any thing—
for there is no person who does not have his hour,
and there is no thing without its place in the sun."

THIS TEACHING TELLS US THAT EVERY SINGLE HUMAN
being in the world and every single thing in the world is worthy
of acknowledgement, good or bad. Everyone and everything has
a place in the world God created and should not be disdained nor
underrated. What an important teaching! This is a worthy goal
and sometimes challenging to attain. It is one that needs constant
attention and awareness. A kind word, a smile, a pat on the back—
literal or spoken—goes a long way in this regard.   *Lois*

✳ *In what ways can we be more accepting of people or things*
   we find annoying or unimportant?

✳ *How would you want to be treated and thought of by*
   others?

Your Wisdom

pIRKEI AVOT 4:6

"Rabbi Yishmael, his [Rabbi Yochanan ben B'roka] son, taught:
A person who studies in order to teach
is given the opportunity both to study and to teach.
A person who studies in order to observe the mitzvot [command-
ments]
is given the opportunity to study, to teach,
to observe the mitzvot and to perform them."

YOU CAN "BE THE CHANGE YOU WANT TO SEE IN THE
world!" (commonly attributed to Gandhi) The idea that actions
speak louder than words is clear from this teaching. We cannot
simply read a parenting book or a how-to book without putting
it into action. Reading this passage makes it clear that we have
a responsibility not just to learn for ourselves, but also to make
action and change in our world.   *Rabbi Posen*

   This passage speaks to our impetus or reason behind the actions
we do.

✻ *What inspires your actions?*

Your Wisdom

pIRKEI AVOT 4:8

"Rabbi Yose taught:
Whoever honors Torah will in turn be honored by others;
whoever dishonors Torah will in turn be dishonored by others."

THIS IS ANOTHER EXAMPLE OF A TEACHING THAT reflects the time in which it was written. To translate it to modern times, I would add the words "the ethical teachings of" to go before the word "Torah" or change the word "Torah" to "ethical behavior," because I do not believe the honor of Torah itself is well enough understood on its own in today's world, but behaving honorably or ethically is. That is what I meant as a mother when I told my children to "Be a *mensch*."   *Lois*

✳ **When you read the word "Torah" in the original text of**
Pirkei Avot, what does it mean to you?

Your Wisdom

pirkei avot 4:10

"This was a favorite teaching of his [Rabbi Yishmael]:
Do not render decisions alone; there is but One who judges alone.
Never say to your colleagues: 'You must adopt my view';
the prerogative is theirs, not yours to coerce."

LIVE IN COMMUNITY; ACT IN COMMUNITY. THE PHRASE
"It takes a village" never rings more true than when looking at
raising a family, building a community, or working toward social
change. Our job is not to change the world on our own, but to
engage with one another, learn from each other, and act with each
other in order to better see all points of view and enact change.
As a parent, I know that I do not have all the answers. I am better
when I share the burden, seek advice, and work together with
my partner and our community. As a rabbi, I know that I cannot
make a decision legally without first engaging in conversation with
others and unpacking all aspects of the situation. Simply put, we
are better together. We are better individuals when we listen to
each other and strengthen one another.   *Rabbi Posen*

✳ *How have you been lifted up by partnership?*

Your Wisdom

pIRKEI AVOT 4:15

"Rabbi Elazar ben Shamua taught:
The dignity of your student
should be as precious to you as your own;
the dignity of your colleague
should be as precious to you as your reverence for your teacher;
your reverence for your teacher
should be as great as your reverence for God."

AS A STUDENT, I ALWAYS WAS MORE INVESTED IN MY learning if my teacher took interest in me as a person, too. We all have something to teach, something to give, something to learn. Treat others as though they are a colleague, a teacher, or a student. Treat one another as if we are all created in God's image and respect the dignity of every human being. I read this as a teacher, a colleague, or a student. I am most likely to learn best with someone who respects me.

Rabbi Posen

✳ **Who else should be added to this list?**

Your Wisdom

pIRKEI AVOT 4:17

"Rabbi Shimon taught:
There are three crowns: The crown of Torah,
The crown of Priesthood, and the crown of Royalty.
The crown of a good name surpasses them all."

WITHOUT THE CROWN OF A GOOD NAME, NO TITLE, NO achievement, no job, no award is worthy of recognition or respect. They are all irrelevant if the person owning them does not have honor and integrity, i.e., does not own the "crown of a good name." As women, teachers, leaders, mothers, it is our job to be constantly aware of our actions and how we behave: to be role models to those around us and to wear the crown of a good name in all endeavors.

Lois

✳ *What kind of qualities does a person need to have to own a "crown of a good name"?*

✳ *How do you think we acquire these qualities?*

Your Wisdom

pIRKEI AVOT 4:18

"Rabbi N'horai taught:
Only with colleagues can your studies by fortified.
Do not rely on your own understanding."

MY PERCEPTION OF THIS TEACHING IS THAT OUR KNOWL-edge is strengthened by learning with others: debating, questioning, discussing the issue, and seeing multiple possibilities. Conversely, learning in solitude may diminish the depth of our learning, limiting our ability to see different possibilities and facets to what is being studied. I find that we women, in particular, often discuss and re-discuss issues and, in so doing, enhance our perception and learning.   *Lois*

✳ *How do you study best?*

Your Wisdom

pirkei avot 4:23

"Rabbi Shimon ben Elazar taught:
Do not pacify your colleague when his anger is raging;
do not comfort him when his dead lies before him;
do not challenge him at the time he makes his vow;
do not intrude upon him at the time of his disgrace."

THIS *MISHNAH* REMINDS US OF THE POWER OF SPACE. There are moments in life when we all need space, whether it is a time-out for a child or an adult who needs to step out of a situation. Our job is to recognize the need both in ourselves and with others so that we can move forward with strength. Sometimes the best thing we can do is to simply give space.   *Rabbi Posen*

✳ *How can another person best support you in each of these scenarios?*

Your Wisdom

PIRKEI AVOT 4:26

"Rabbi Yose bar Y'hudah of K'far Bavli taught:
To what may we compare one who learns from the young?
To one who eats unripe grapes and drinks from the vat.
To what may we compare one who learns from the old?
To one who eats ripe grapes and drinks wine that is aged."

THIS PASSAGE SUGGESTS THAT LEARNING FROM THE OLD is a thing of value and learning from the young is not. While I very much agree with the value of learning from the old with their wisdom of experience, I disagree 100 percent with regard to learning from the young. As a parent and teacher, I know for certain that learning from the young is a thing of value. In addition to the learning imparted, there is value in teaching the young by example that their opinions are worthy in and of themselves. Some of the most important lessons I have learned have come from my children and from students with whom I have worked.   *Lois*

✳ *Do you agree or disagree with the viewpoint expressed in this mishnah?*

✳ *Why or why not?*

✳ *What do you think prompted this point of view?*

[Author's note: This book, *Pirkei Imahot: The Wisdom of Mothers, The Voices of Women*, and the study that preceded it, provide the antithesis of this teaching since Rabbi Posen is 45 years younger than I, and I have learned from her consistently throughout the entire process. She is more learned than I in Jewish knowledge, while I have more experiential knowledge than she. We have different perspectives and outlooks, and we learn from one another with mutual respect.]

Your Wisdom

PIRKEI AVOT 5:15

"There are four types among those who give tz'dakah [philanthropy]:
Those who want to give but do not want others to give—
they begrudge their fellow human beings the mitzvah [command-
ment];
those who want others to give but refuse themselves to give—
they are miserly;
those who want to give and also want others to give—
they are saintly;
those who do not want others to give and themselves do not give—
they are scoundrels."

THIS PASSAGE SAYS IT LIKE IT IS. BUT, WHAT I LIKE MOST
about this teaching is that it can be applied to so many other *mitz-*
vot (commandments) as well, with the change of just a few words.
Try substituting different words at the end of the first sentence.
For example: There are four types who "give service," "who vote,"
"who care for others," "who give of their time," "who take leadership roles" and on and on and on. You can make up new words
to describe who *they* are at the end of the four descriptions, and it
works. Hopefully, when you evaluate who you are in the process,
you will be able to call yourself "saintly" in this context.   *Lois*

✳ *What words might you substitute at the end of the first*
   sentence in this teaching to change the meaning to one of
   more relevance to you?

✳ *What can you do to help yourself belong to the "saintly"*
   category?

YOUR WISDOM

pIRKEI AVOT 5:23

"This was another favorite teaching of his [Yehudah ben Tema]:
At the age of five—the study of Bible; at ten—the study of Mishnah;
at thirteen—responsibility for the mitzvot;
At fifteen—the study of Talmud; at eighteen—marriage;
at twenty—pursuit of a livelihood;
at thirty—the peak of one's powers;
at forty—the age of understanding; at fifty—the age of counsel;
at sixty—old age; at seventy—the hoary head;
at eighty—the age of 'strength'; at ninety—the bent back;
at one hundred—as one dead and out of this world."

As Ecclesiastes teaches, "There is a time to every *purpose under heaven."* So often we have a quest to know it all only to learn that we have to be patient and learn in the time and place that is right for us. This *mishnah* reminds me that, as we age, our interests and understandings change. What we see as the world at two is certainly not how we will see the world at five, ten, or fifteen years old. The important lesson is that we continue to learn, continue to evolve, and continue to grow as human beings.

Rabbi Posen

✳ *When you compare the interests that you had five years ago with your current interests, what surprises you the most?*

Your Wisdom

pIRKEI AVOT 5:24

"Ben Bag-Bag taught:
Study it and review it—you will find everything in it.
Scrutinize it, grow old and gray in it, do not depart from it.
There is no better portion of life than this."

THIS IS THE REASONING FOR READING THE TORAH OVER and over again each year. Just as you might read your favorite book again and again and find new meanings and values in it each time, so, too, we do with the Torah. Ben Bag-Bag recognizes that review is essential for growth, new understanding, and truly unlocking the magic in the world. As the parent of a toddler who wants to read the same book over and over and over again, I can appreciate this point of view since each time we find a new character, story, or lesson to talk about.

Rabbi Posen

✳ *What joy do you find in repetition?*

✳ *Can there be growth without repetition?*

Your Wisdom

PIRKEI IMAHOT

Introducing
Pirkei Imahot

When we named our book *Pirkei Imahot*, we chose two subtitles: *The Wisdom of Mothers* and *The Voices of Women*. We chose both because each is important. This section of the book reflects that choice.

The wisdom of mothers, usually our first teachings in life, often helps to form who we are as adults. These teachings are not to be taken lightly. Rather, they are to be honored and cherished as the foundation of our ethical behavior and the transmitters of our values.

The same is true of **the voices of women**. In today's world, women have a voice: a voice we use to stand up and be counted and a voice to which we listen. At this moment in history, our voices—the voices of women—are being heard more strongly than ever before. We hope our book will increase the importance of those voices in the Jewish world.

So what do we do with these voices that teach us lessons or give us pride in our heritage? How do we use them? It is up to each of us to find ways to use the inspiration they provide to do the right thing—to pursue justice, keep an open mind, and help bring about change where change is needed.

The New York Times best-selling author Barbara De Angelis said, "Women need real moments of solitude and self-reflection to balance out how much of ourselves we give away." We hope this section of our book will provide such moments for you and give you inspiration, strength, and purpose as you move forward to better our world.

The words of wisdom that follow were contributed by Jewish women from across America. We have placed each contribution into one of five broad categories to reflect what we thought was the contributor's primary focus. The five categories in this section are related to our areas of interest. Many contributions could have gone into more than one category. We have also supplemented this section with quotes from well-known Jewish women.

SECTION ONE

FIRST THINGS FIRST

CHAPTER ONE
Getting Started

Diana Ayton-Shenker, social innovator, impact strategist

AN AFRICAN HUMAN RIGHTS LEADER ONCE TAUGHT ME how his path became clear as he was struggling to bring justice to his country. Suddenly he realized, *what we hold in our hands is a compass*. We each hold in our hands a moral compass to steer us along our ethical path, to align and infuse our behavior with values, to chart our course and lead a life of *Values in Action*.

Consider four core directions as cardinal compass points: Inspiration, Intention, Integrity, and Impact. They offer guideposts of daily life and pose fundamental questions: When do I receive and share *inspiration*? How do I set *intention*? Am I clear in my vision? Do I approach and embody *integrity* in my words and actions? Do I value my positive *impact* and cultivate my capacity to make a difference in our world?

Let your *Values in Action* compass guide your way as you strive to prioritize with gratitude, pursue justice and keep an open mind, listen to those who need to be heard, speak up when your voice adds wisdom or kindness, do the right thing, and help repair the world.

Miriam Baumgartner, full-time volunteer, leader

"First things first!" – my mother

NOT NECESSARILY JEWISH, NOT NECESSARILY PROFOUND, but a very simple way to determine what is truly important. I quote her frequently.

For Further Reflection

✳ *What values might you choose to put on the four points of your own moral compass?*

✳ *If you were to list the things that make up "first things first" in your life, what would they be?*

✳ *Have they changed over time?*

Your Wisdom

chapter two
Setting Priorities

Denise Handlarski, rabbi, teacher, mother

THERE IS NO WORK MORE PROFOUND AND MORE CHALlenging than the work of motherhood. It is a grind, and it is elation; it is the soul and the conflation of all of our other roles. It is an identity, not a vocation. And, yet, there is other work to be done: work in the home and work in our communities. We work as teachers, as rabbis, as nurses, as engineers. The work does not cease to be meaningful or fulfilling once we become mothers. And, if we do not do this work, who will fix our schools, our bridges, our communities? Who will show our daughters what it is to be strong, to be needed, to be oneself? We need women and mothers to do all kinds of work. But more than that, we need to occupy every field so that mothers are the voices of reason and compassion everywhere—so the world grows more healthfully, and, therefore, so do all of our children.

Laura Kosak, therapist, life coach

GOD WAS OUR FIRST MINDFULNESS TEACHER. IN A LIMinal moment between emotion and action, before the choice of murder, God speaks to Cain, *"Why are you so distressed? ... Surely, if you do right, there is uplift. But if you do not do right, sin crouches at the door, its urge is toward you, yet you can be its master."* (Genesis 4:6-7). It is a strange and compelling verse—a powerful metaphor for the very human struggle between good and evil. Notice that

PIRKEI IMAHOT

Cain is not commanded to avoid wrong, rather he is invited to choose right. If sin, as we understand in Judaism, is missing the mark, like an archer, then God is holding open the space between potential and action, encouraging Cain to pause and aim well, to consider and then to act. Choice—the options live within us. We will always be called by misdirected possibilities—that is what it means to have a choice that matters. Our greatness lies in our choice. Pause, plant your feet on the ground, take aim toward your greatest self, and release.

Salem Pearce, rabbinical student, book lover

WHEN I WAS TRYING TO DECIDE WHETHER TO GO TO rabbinical school, I spoke with my grandmother, *z"l* (may she be remembered as a blessing), regarding my concerns about the length of the program. "Granny Gay," I said, "If I go back to school, I'll be almost 40 by the time I'm a rabbi." She looked at me with a smile. "But, you're going to be 40 anyway. You might as well be doing what you want to do." (I am currently in rabbinical school, doing what I want to do.)

Caron Blau Rothstein, Jewish professional leader

"The purpose of life is not to be happy. It is to be useful, to be honorable, to be compassionate, to have it make some difference that you have lived and lived well." – Ralph Waldo Emerson

WHILE I DIDN'T SAY THESE WORDS, THEY REALLY ENCAP-sulate how I try to live and how I try to raise my kids to live their lives.

For Further Reflection

✳ *How do you go about setting priorities?*

✳ *What do you think is the most important part of parenting?*

✳ *If, in fact, God gives us choice, in what ways have you used that choice in the past?*

✳ *How might you use that choice in the future?*

Your Wisdom

CHAPTER THREE
What Really Counts

Sheri Cordova, Jewish professional, mother, grandmother

"Who is wise? One who foresees the future consequences of his acts." – Babylonian Talmud, Tamid 32a

FROM THIS WE LEARN THAT "EVERYTHING COUNTS." Words that are spoken, relationships we engage in, behaviors which we model, messages we write, even body language and facial expressions are capable of leaving an indelible impression on the recipient which may be remembered in ways that can influence self-esteem or decisions made.

We have no way of knowing if and when our behavior will indeed have an effect—which word of encouragement will set someone on a course of achievement, which raised eyebrow will crush the enthusiasm.

Our responsibility is to be sensitive in what we say and do—aware that we have the potential to influence someone's emotional well-being or sense of self-confidence. When we sincerely care about other people, we will enter into relationships with humility and sensitivity.

We honor our commitment to *Hashem* (another name for God) by interacting with others with love and mutual respect, by remembering that "EVERYTHING COUNTS."

Lois Shenker, author, teacher, life coach, mother, grandmother

TWO WEEKS BEFORE MY WEDDING, 56 YEARS AGO, MY mother and I were standing in the guest room of the home in which I was raised, looking over the wedding gifts on display there. As we were commenting on one item or another, she turned to me and said, "I want to ask you a question. If the Queen of England came to visit, would you use your finest things?"

"Of course I would!" I replied.

And then she looked at me with a wistful smile and said, "Honey, she's not coming. Use your finest things for your family. You will never have more important company!"

I have lived by that wisdom ever since.

Susan Turnbull, immediate past chair of Jewish Council for Public Affairs, mother, grandmother

"YOU ARE THE WEALTHIEST FAMILY I KNOW," MY TEEN-age cousin Ellen once told my mom. Growing up, my dad drove a cab, and my mother worked in a department store. We rented the downstairs of a two family house. Ellen drove a convertible and lived in a big house. What she saw as valuable was what *we* had: our family just loved each other, and we had fun.

In our home, there never was a quote from a book, a poem, or a family saying that was often repeated. We didn't have words to live by on a needlepoint pillow or a placard in the kitchen, but Ellen's comment was repeated for decades with pride. We were rich because we had each other. That's all we ever really needed. It is all anyone really needs—people to love and to be loved.

My best lifetime lesson is really very simple: love and be loved. As has been said before, *"The rest is commentary."*

For Further Reflection

﹡ *What is really important to you in terms of family?*

﹡ *In terms of career?*

﹡ *In terms of activism?*

﹡ *In terms of personal development?*

﹡ *In terms of spirituality?*

﹡ *How do you show people what is important to you?*

﹡ *How do you help nurture what is important to others in your life?*

Your Wisdom

Chapter Four

Jewish Identity/ Spirituality

Mychal Copeland, rabbi

WHY FRET OVER THE QUESTION, "DO YOU BELIEVE IN God?" The most important question about your spiritual life is not whether or not you are a believer, but whether or not you are a seeker. This over-asked and overly simplistic question elicits a one-word answer of "yes" or "no" that tells very little about who we are and what is important to us. Rather, spend time every day pondering the profound questions that reveal who you are: Why are we here? Why am I here? What is my purpose? How do I make life feel sacred? Who am I in the face of the enormity of the universe?

Call it God. Don't call it God. That is not what matters. The goal of existence should be to live in awe of the grandeur of life and death. Every day is filled with large and small moments that could be marked as sacred if we simply notice them. Amidst the busyness of everyday existence, slow down long enough to be allowed a glimpse of something deeper: the magnificence, the terrifying immensity of it all.

Carol Danish, community volunteer, mother, grandmother

IN 1999, AFTER 22 YEARS OF KIDNEY DISEASE, MY FUTURE health was dependent upon the choice between dialysis and a potential transplant. Thankfully, I was able to receive a healthy kidney from my daughter Debra.

When I woke up in the ICU following surgery and after learning my daughter was recovering well, I looked at the beautiful day outside and began to cry. I turned to the nurse and said, "Look at the sky. It is bluer than I have ever seen it before. And, the grass is so very green. God is telling me that I have a new life and a new season." It was the most intense and beautiful day of my life, one where I felt absolutely full of purpose.

I have been able to see many things, both happy and sad, in the years since I received my new kidney. I know that when life brings us pain and suffering and difficult times, we often look to God for assistance or comfort. What I believe is even more important, however, is loving and appreciating God on an everyday basis when all is good, when we feel free and joyous, and when it is a beautiful day.

Marla Feldman, rabbi, executive director of Women of Reform Judaism

"KNOW BEFORE WHOM YOU STAND." SOMETIMES DURING worship, I pause and reflect when I see these words above the ark. I wonder what the world would be like if we really believed we stood before God at all times. How would we act if we knew our actions would always be seen?

I recall a scene in the movie *The Truman Show*, when the unwitting subject of a television show slowly becomes aware he is being watched. Gazing in a mirror, he has a growing sense that others see him. Imagine what we might do, or not do, if nothing went unseen.

How would we live our lives if we knew every action would be witnessed? Perhaps that is the role of God in modern society, not

Aristotle's "Unmoved Mover," but rather our "Unwatched Watcher," who sees us even when others do not. We don't have the option to press the cosmic off switch or turn off our video screen when we stand before the One Who sees all. And knowing we are seen, what choices will we make?

Denise Handlarski, rabbi, teacher, mother

THE WOMEN KNOW THAT WE AS A PEOPLE WILL ALWAYS struggle with what it means to be part of our people, for we birth and raise the people, our people, in each generation. We are the people consumed with wandering and wondering. We are the ones always in search of, restless, and obsessed with our own becoming. And then, ultimately, we are born or reborn or we find a home. This search, of being and becoming, is the Jewish search. Our strivings as individuals mirror the strivings of our people: we are never still, we are never one, and, yet, we are united in our quest for longing and belonging.

Irene Hecht, retired academic

I FIND THAT WHEN I TELL PEOPLE I AM "A JEW BY choice," the next question is usually, "When did you convert?" My response to this inquiry has two parts. The first is that I never converted, which seems to me to suggest that one day I was A and the next I became B. Second, I try to suggest that every Jew is a convert, beginning with our esteemed father Abraham.

To be Jewish is a matter of seeking to live according to certain standards, of which justice is one of the most important. It assumes we care for other human beings and for our environment. For some, it involves a roster of dos and don'ts. What is on the roster is our responsibility. There is no deity who can excuse us when we drift in a poorly chosen direction. It is up to us to recognize that fact and to change direction.

Gerda Weissmann Klein, Holocaust survivor, author

OUR FAMILY'S MOST FAVORITE SAYING IS INSPIRED BY my mother Helen Weissmann's advice: *"Don't ask God to give you what you pray for—but only what is good for you."* It has become our guideline in life.

Lori Shapiro, rabbi, artistic director

A WISE WOMAN ONCE TOLD ME: "I DON'T KNOW WHAT God is. I don't even know that God is; but, I do know that when I look for something with curiosity and an open mind, I am bound to find something in the search."

Deborah Waxman, rabbi, communal leader

AS I STRIVE TO LIVE AND LEAD WITH HUMILITY AND effectiveness, I frequently meditate on the image of a *kli kodesh* (a vessel of holiness). The Torah refers to the implements used in the ancient Temple as *kley kodesh* (plural of *kli kodesh*). Over the centuries, the term has come to refer to rabbis and other leaders who serve the Jewish people. In my mind's eye, sometimes the *kli* (vessel) is my work, and sometimes I am the *kli*.

However I imagine it, the vessel is always a cup: wide-bottomed and sturdy, with stable walls that can be filled with, well, anything.

When I am the vessel, I focus on the stability of the cup's walls and the sense of expansiveness they create. When my work is the vessel, I focus on filling the expanse with *kedushah* (holiness) and a sense of *avodah* (service) and letting these flow through me and into the world. In both instances, I try to infuse my meditation with a sense of abundance and gratitude, chanting over and over *"kosi revayah"* (my cup is overflowing) (Psalm 23:5).

For Further Reflection

✻ *How do you respond to this challenge posed in the first entry of this chapter?*

"*Spend time every day pondering the profound questions that reveal who you are: Why are we here? Why am I here? What is my purpose? How do I make life feel sacred? Who am I in the face of the enormity of the universe?*"

✻ *How would you live your life if you knew every one of your actions would be witnessed?*

✻ *How might your behavior change from what it is now?*

One contributor in this section wrote:

"*To be Jewish is a matter of seeking to live according to certain standards, of which justice is one of the most important.*"

✻ *Do you agree or disagree?*

✻ *What do you do to remind yourself to behave in ways that affirm your values?*

Your Wisdom

CHAPTER FIVE

Motivation/ Gratitude

Marni Fogulson, writer

EVERY NIGHT BEFORE I GO TO SLEEP, I SILENTLY SAY, "Thank you for this blessing of a day." As a result of losing loved ones and being ill myself, I know that each day, even if it is filled with tribulations, is a gift and an opportunity to be the mother and human I want to be.

Deborah Meyer, leader, community builder, mother

IT IS SOMETIMES HARD TO ASK FOR WHAT YOU WANT, but if you don't ask, you won't receive. This is true in every sphere of our lives, and it is often especially hard for women, according to research and in my experience.

We can be frustrated that other people don't seem to know what we want and need. We can be angry they don't step forward and provide for us—emotionally, spiritually, or physically, with love and affection, a change in behavior, or a pay raise. However, if we don't ask, how will they know what we want?

In an old joke, every night Minnie prays to win the lottery. Near death, she asks God why, since she has lived such a pure life and prayed for it every night, she has not yet won. God replies, "Minnie, help me out—buy a ticket!"

Asking clearly and without apology is like buying the ticket. We don't always win, but at least we have set in motion the possibility that we will.

Lois Shenker, author, teacher, life coach, mother, grandmother

A LESSON FROM MY 6TH GRADE TEACHER WHO MADE US memorize this poem:
"Good, better, best,
Take no rest.
Till your good is better,
And your better is best."

Amee Huppin Sherer, Jewish educator, director of University of Washington Hillel, mother

"Charismatic leaders make us think, 'Oh, if only I could do that, be like that.' True leaders make us think, 'If they can do that, then…I can too.'" – John Holt, educator

I HAVE BEEN BLESSED TO WITNESS GREAT LEADERSHIP over the years. Each time I encountered someone in a leadership position, I internalized new things I saw within myself. Amongst these leaders were camp counselors, United Synagogue Youth regional and international board members, friends, family members, and favorite teachers.

As I began my own teaching career, I often told my students, "I will tell you what to do, but how you do it is up to you." I was always inspired by how differently children would interpret assignments based on their own skills and interests. Working now with college students, I am honored to witness them finding their own voices as they struggle with injustices and make choices to improve our world. I aspire to be the kind of leader who inspires each of them to embrace their own unique gifts and talents, so they can lead the next generation with confidence.

For Further Reflection

* *What motivates you and gets you going?*

* *What keeps you going when you become frustrated or discouraged?*

* *What place does gratitude have in your life?*

* *Is it something you reflect on consciously, frequently, occasionally, seldom?*

* *Do people who matter in your life know what you appreciate about them?*

* *How can you show them?*

Your Wisdom

SECTION TWO

Tzedek, Tzedek Tirdof: Justice, Justice Shall Thou Pursue

chapter one

Pursuing Justice

Deborah Kolodny, rabbi, non-profit executive director, spiritual director

Pirkei Avot 2:16

"Rabbi Tarfon taught: It is not your responsibility to finish the work, but neither are you free to desist from it."

THIS TEACHING ASKS US THE QUESTION, HOW MUCH IS enough? We say YES to every need, and we sacrifice ourselves, resulting in adrenal and/or chronic fatigue, depression or anxiety, fibromyalgia, sleepless nights.

We read in *Bereshit* (Genesis) how Avraham's hand was stayed just as he was about to sacrifice his son. No matter how surely Avraham, or we, thinks God wants human sacrifice, that is most surely not the case.

Today it is hard to hear God's voice. *HaShem's* angels might be shouting at us: "ENOUGH!" But, we can't hear through all the noise and all the busyness.

But, this teaching comes through loud and clear: work for human rights and racial justice, tend to children, be extraordinary professionals, care for the hearts of coworkers, nourish primary relationships. And, always remember: God does not ask for human sacrifice.

Jodi Kornfeld, humanistic Jewish rabbi

LEVITICUS 19:14'S INJUNCTION NOT TO PUT A STUM-
bling block before the blind or not to curse the deaf is ironic
since the blind cannot see who did such a thing nor can the deaf
hear what was said. But we will know if we have done such things,
diminishing the world by such acts. The idea that each of us can
make a difference to improve the world in big and small ways is a
fundamental principle of our tradition.

Collectively, we accomplish much, but it is what the individual
can do that matters. We are empowered to make a difference and
have the ability to achieve change. We can assume responsibility
for the Judaism that reflects our values, families, and lives. We
can educate our children in a meaningful and relevant way that
treasures Jewish culture. We can engage in holiday celebrations that
enhance our Jewish identity. There is great power in this and great
responsibility. There is no one else who can make these decisions
for us. It is up to us.

Beth Reisbard, educator, fund raiser

WE ARE COMMANDED TO BE A LIGHT UNTO THE NATIONS.
These few words continue to be my constant guide—seeking to be
a source of light, inspiration, and hope in my daily interactions.
Often, our actions and priorities are role models for our families
as well as for those we connect with in the community or at work.
I remind myself that none of us has walked in another's shoes,
know their story, or feel their pain. Looking in another human's
eyes inspires me to see their light, goodness, and *neshama* (soul).

For Further Reflection

✳ *What does pursuing justice mean to you?*

✳ *How do you know when you have completed your work?*

✳ *How can you, as an individual, affect change?*

✳ *How do you inspire others to pursue justice and affect change?*

CHAPTER TWO
A Woman's Voice

Nancy Kaufman, feminist, social justice activist, CEO of National Council of Jewish Women [NCJW]

"Who is this 'new' woman? She is the woman who dares to go into the world and do what her convictions demand."
– Hannah G. Solomon, founder of NCJW 1893

INSPIRED BY NCJW'S FOUNDER, NCJW WOMEN STILL are in the world living their values and taking action to advance social change. As our foremothers believed almost 125 years ago, we still believe it is our responsibility *"to correct social injustice and combat the lack of humanism."*

Lynn Magid Lazar, full-time volunteer

THE NECESSITY FOR WOMEN TO WORK TOGETHER—THE need for sisterhood—is great. Whether it is human rights, education, Jewish literacy, or social justice—the need is tremendous. There are issues others may not address if we, as women, do not tackle them. There are concerns that may never be focused on if we, as women, do not undertake them. There are moments and relationships that can be lost in the blur of activity if we, as women, do not value them.

Magic happens when women come together. We laugh and share our tears. We study Torah in different ways and tell our own stories. We break bread together (and chocolate). We go shopping for our first *tallit* (prayer shawl), and we take clothing to homeless shelters. We understand that relationships are key. In challenging and confusing times in our history, we need each other more than ever. We create community because living in isolation in an imperfect world is much too challenging. Our collective power is unstoppable.

Elizabeth Steiner Hayward, state senator in Oregon

REJOICE IN BEING A WOMAN, AND NEVER LET ANYONE define you or what you can or should do by your gender. Have faith in your abilities, your wisdom, your style, and don't succumb to criticism without serious consideration. Within a pretty broad range of reason, behave in ways that fit who you are, regardless of whether others think it's a "male" way to behave.

For Further Reflection

✳ *Have there been times when you have felt uplifted or strengthened by the power of joining forces with other women?*

✳ *If so, what were they?*

✳ *How do you appreciate being you?*

✳ *In what ways can you recognize and support the voices of the important people in your life?*

chapter three
Keeping An Open Mind

Susan Averbach, writer, rabbi, grandmother
Pirkei Avot 4:1

"Ben Zoma would say: 'Who is wise? One who learns from every man.'"

I HAVE SEEN THE WORD "MAN" EXPAND TO THE WORD "person" in my lifetime—and I believe we can all learn from every person: man, woman, child, Jewish, Christian, Muslim, Buddhist. We must break out of our boundaries that are born of fear and chauvinism and learn from each other. Our world depends on it!

Gloria Borg Olds, retired bookstore co-owner, grandmother

WHAT IS AN OPEN MIND? TO ME, IT IS THE DESIRE AND ability not to close ourselves off to people, ideas, or experiences. Many of us do not often associate with a diverse group of people. Economically, ethnically, or religiously, our associations may be limited.

If I don't have a friend who struggles to put food on the table, I may not truly understand the difficulties of a person who does. If I worship in a religious community that teaches, even with subtle messages, that a particular religion is better than other choices, I may not appreciate why others worship in different ways or not at all. If my sexual orientation is toward the opposite sex, I may not understand the attraction to the same sex. If my family was born in this country, I may not appreciate the struggles of immigration.

What makes all differences understandable, and thus leads to mutual respect, is keeping an open mind. How to teach and encourage an open mind is a topic worthy of frequent discussion, and I do believe it is a habit of mind that directly leads to the pursuit of social justice.

For Further Reflection

✳ *Who has been the most "unlikely teacher" in your life?*

✳ *How do you define an open mind?*

Your Wisdom

SECTION THREE

ETHICAL BEHAVIOR

CHAPTER ONE
Doing The Right Thing

Carmella Abraham, MD, Yeshivat Maharat student

Pirkei Avot 4:1

"Ben Azzai used to say: 'Do not be scornful of any person and do not be disdainful of anything—for you have no person without its hour and no thing without its place.'"

SYNAGOGUES ASPIRE TO BUILD SACRED COMMUNITIES. However, strongly held opinions shared at *shul* (Yiddish word for synagogue) committee meetings can sometimes divide people, irrevocably altering friendships. My mother modeled for me the importance of moving past the differences we may have with others.

In truth, it would take me years to internalize my mother's lessons. I recall once arguing a sensitive point with a good friend. Later, I wondered if I had inadvertently hurt our friendship, but I was afraid to approach her to make amends. Years later, I would come home from my mother's funeral to find, to my surprise, that my dear friend was there to greet me and had set up my house: covering the mirrors, arranging the food, and setting up the chairs. I was grateful for her gift of moving beyond the past. My friend had built a bridge forward for us, much like my mother would have done, bolstering our friendship and healing old wounds instantly—a divine gesture, a profound blessing, a sacred community.

Jenn Director Knudsen, writer, Francophile, mother

I GREW UP IN A THERAPY-PHOBIC HOUSEHOLD. SO WHEN I took my eldest child, then six, to a therapist, it was a very hard day for me because I had to admit that she required help.

Mornings went smoothly, but then she would lose the ability to cope as the afternoon dragged into evening. Her increasingly frenetic behavior communicated that noises got increasingly loud; others' movements became too unpredictable; her attention span decreased while her meltdowns rocketed; even our house cat appeared menacing to her.

Within ten minutes of our first session, the doctor diagnosed GAD (generalized anxiety disorder). A couple years later, as my daughter revealed more about herself and her daily struggles, the diagnosis was Asperger's Syndrome. Now that was a hard day—a new prescription, social-skills classes, provision of increasing emotional scaffolding.

But, I had to make proper choices for the family my husband and I created. Today, at 15, my daughter is empathic; copes appropriately with fraught experiences; loves learning about herself and others—and, she dreams of becoming a mother herself one day.

Elizabeth Steiner Hayward, state senator in Oregon

TRY HARD TO ALWAYS TAKE THE HIGH ROAD. IT IS SO tempting to return snark to snark, to be mean when we are hurt, to speak before we think when we are in the heat of the moment. But afterward, you will regret those words and actions. Yes, you will burn a little inside when you bite your tongue. But then you will glow more from the sense you behaved in ways you can be proud of.

As a parent, trust yourself and your children enough to say, "I don't know how to be a good parent to you right now." Kids need to understand that adults don't know everything, that we're willing to learn, and that saying "I don't know" is OK. Also, consider putting yourself in "time-out" if you feel yourself losing your cool. This teaches kids self-regulation. These techniques particularly help during moments of intense emotion, when we need ways to step back.

For Further Reflection

* *Describe what ethical behavior means to you.*

* *What is the hardest part of moving past differences with others?*

* *Recognizing we need help can be difficult. How can you move past recognition into action?*

CHAPTER TWO
Ethical Guidelines For Daily Living

Mychal Copeland, rabbi

WHICH IS MORE IMPORTANT: STRUGGLING TO MEND OUR broken world or appreciating what we have been given? We cannot do one without the other.

The Jewish people are given two names in the Torah. Leah names her fourth son Yehuda, "gratitude." *"Yehudim"* means "Jews," or more literally, "the thankful ones." Jacob struggles with an angel who bestows upon him a new name, "Yisrael," meaning "struggles with God." We are wrestlers. We will fight until dawn and not despair, no matter how bleak it looks.

How can we be both the thankful ones, grateful for what is, and also be the ones who struggle because it isn't good enough? How do we live in awe of life if it is also in our nature to say, "This world should be better"? We must be comfortable living in the paradox.

It has been suggested: a person should carry in each pocket a slip of paper with one of our names. One reads, "I am Yehuda: I am grateful for what is," while the other reads, "I am Yisrael: I will always fight to make it better."

Erica Goldman, Jewish educator/teacher, mother

IN THE SPIRIT OF THE ENDURING WISDOM OF *PIRKEI Avot*, I offer here the primary guiding principles I try to live by. They apply to all areas of life. As with *Pirkei Avot*, they are pithy and invite ongoing commentary. I believe the best commentary is in the living.

1. Always ask "What is my purpose?"
2. Assume it is possible to have "I-Thou" dialogue with every human being, as we are all created *b'tzelem Elohim* (in God's image).
3. Recognize that diversity exists within unity.
4. Work from the inside out—take care of those closest to you first.
5. Remember that we are ambassadors for the Jewish people in everything we do, and we have the capacity to influence for the good through our actions and our speech.
6. Jewish living is the same as living. We should try to sanctify every day in the smallest of actions.

My parents taught me to live honestly and ethically. My husband is an ongoing living example of *tocho k'varo* (the inside is like the outside). They are instrumental in helping me develop a way to approach living with purpose and meaning.

Abby Levine, director of Jewish Social Justice Roundtable, mother

"When I dare to be powerful, to use my strength in service of my vision, then it becomes less and less important whether I am afraid." – Audre Lorde

Deborah Meyer, leader, community builder, mother

IN THE COURSE OF BUILDING AN ORGANIZATION, I HAVE learned very deeply how much we need each other. For a natural born and raised perfectionist, this is liberating.

In my organization, we each have a job description, a list of all of the things we are supposed to do. The reality is that each of us, including me, is really great at doing most of our jobs, but not all of our jobs. There are some aspects of the job we really don't enjoy or we are not so great at doing. The good news is that we are also often interested in and skilled at something that someone else is supposed to be doing.

Ideally, as an organization, we fit together tongue and groove. We are all rolling forward toward our shared vision, with each of us doing much ourselves, helping each other, and being helped by those around us. And, in this way, we are an almost perfect union of coworkers.

Sura Rubenstein, writer

BE KIND, BE GENEROUS, BE HUMBLE. STRIVE TO LIVE your life with integrity. Avoid rushing to judgment; remember that we often do not see a whole picture. And remember, too, that every person has something to contribute to the world.

Lois Shenker, author, teacher, life coach, mother, grandmother

MY MOTHER-IN-LAW HAD TWO SAYINGS SHE LIVED BY and quoted often. The first was, *"Cast your bread upon the waters,"* (Ecclesiastes 11:1) which was her way of saying, "Do the right thing and look out for others." The quote actually continues with the words "for you will find it after many days." Her unspoken corollary from these words was that this was the price one should pay to be rewarded with a good life in return.

The second saying was from Shakespeare's play, *Hamlet*: "*To thine own self be true, and it must follow, as the night the day, thou canst not then be false to any man.*" She not only lived by this herself, but expected it of her children and quoted it to her grandchildren as well.

For Further Reflection

✳ *What is the best way you know to teach values to children?*

✳ *To students?*

✳ *To contemporaries?*

From the first contributor in chapter two:

> "*Which is more important, struggling to mend our broken world or appreciating what we have been given?*"

✳ *Why do you think so?*

✳ *What is your purpose?*

✳ *What is your skill set?*

✳ *What one ethical lesson have you taught/will teach others?*

Your Wisdom

CHAPTER THREE
Teaching Values

Irene Hecht, retired academic

MY MOTHER WAS FOND OF RECITING TO ME A GUIDE TO living which said, "A place for everything and everything in its place." I suspect its motivation was a desire to see that my bedroom did not become a hazardous clutter of toys and discarded clothing. However, over the years, it has gained a measure of wisdom for me and a standard highly compatible with basic Jewish values. We have a daunting list of 613 *mitzvot* (commandments). Although only 271 are relevant today, Jews rarely, if ever, manage to adhere to them. What remains, however, is a profound sense that there are principles to our lives and that it is up to each of us to identify and adhere to those principles.

Suzi Levy, health worker

A TEACHER ONCE POINTED OUT THAT NO ONE BELIEVES they are a bad person. This thought helps me to have compassion and perspective. It helps me to humanize those with whom I'm angry. It causes less emotional suffering to question the thoughts of those who hurt me and more emotional suffering to feel anger at being the target of a bad person.

Fern Winkler Schlesinger, community leader, educator, philanthropist, mother

ONE OF THE THINGS I ALWAYS REMEMBER BEING TOLD as a child is that in this world other people can take almost everything away from you, but there are two things only you yourself can destroy. One is your education, so get the most from it, and the other is your word. Always be honest, trustworthy, and truthful. When people know that is your character, they will believe in what you say and what you do and then they, too, will follow you.

FOR FURTHER REFLECTION

✳ *How do compassion and perspective play a role in your life?*

SECTION FOUR

TZEDAKAH AND TIKKUN OLAM

CHAPTER ONE

Philanthropy

Renee Holzman, philanthropist, mother, grandmother

"I expect to pass through this world but once; any good thing therefore that I can do, or any kindness that I can show to any fellow creature, let me do it now; let me not defer or neglect it, for I shall not pass this way again."

— Quaker saying, sometimes attributed to Stephen Grellet

THIS QUOTE ESPECIALLY RESONATES WITH ME BECAUSE it is the way my mother and father lived their lives. When I found this quote tucked in a book after my father died, I realized, though it was unspoken by them, my parents saw the example it suggests as the ultimate good. They lived these precepts and, by example, passed them on to me. It so clearly expresses the goals we wanted to achieve in The Holzman Foundation, created in 1990 by my husband and me, that I chose this quote to define our purpose in directing our philanthropy.

Priscilla Kostiner, professional volunteer

AS I CHAIRED OUR COMMUNITY'S ANNUAL CAMPAIGN, my mantra was, "No matter how much we raise, it is never enough." When the money raised in that campaign had to be allocated, over and over I found myself thinking, "Solomon had it easy—he only had to suggest dividing the baby in two." And finally, after the money was allocated, the thought was, "If you follow those dollars to the end of their journey, you will find a smiling face." What we do most certainly makes a difference in the lives of others.

Fern Winkler Schlesinger, community leader, educator, philanthropist, mother

AS THE CHILD OF TWO HOLOCAUST SURVIVORS, I WAS not brought up with the shadow of the Holocaust looming overhead, but I was cognizant of communal and social responsibility. I watched how my parents helped when they saw a need, how they helped other newcomers to the community, helped create a day school, and helped build a shul. I realized that all of the benefits I enjoyed (day school, B'Nai B'rith Youth Organization) and even how my parents were helped when they first arrived in America, were due to the infrastructure and work of the previous generations. Even as an adolescent, I always believed that, "If you have the ability, you have the responsibility."

Carolyn Weinstein, realtor, community volunteer

I BELIEVE LIFE IS A PRECIOUS AND SACRED GIFT. TO LIVE life without meaning, without purpose, without making a difference, is to deny that gift. Many of us are rich with blessings beyond belief. Yes, our lives have their share of problems and tragedies, yet most of us are vastly blessed with enough to eat, a place to sleep, and the ability to make choices to shape our lives.

When we share our bounty, whether financial or a gift of time and energy, it is as if it were offered on God's altar. All offerings given from the heart, big or small, are counted. We give to those who benefit now and for generations to come. Whether we know the recipients or not, we know that giving generously for *tikkun olam* makes a difference in our lives and the lives of others.

FOR FURTHER REFLECTION

✳ *Have there been times when you look back and regret decisions made or not made?*

✳ *Do you remember times when your giving made an impact?*

One contributor in this chapter wrote:

"If you have the ability, you have the responsibility."

✳ *How does this resonate with you?*

✳ *How might you make a difference in your community?*

CHAPTER TWO

Giving of Yourself

Sandey Soble Fields, daughter, mother, grandmother

MY GRANDMOTHERS CAME TO THIS COUNTRY TO OFFER opportunities for their children. In their Yiddish accents, they taught me their wisdom and their pride in being Jewish in America.

Everything my Russian-born mother taught me was a lesson in being a good person. For example:

1. "If you can't say something nice, don't say anything at all."
2. "Giving from the heart is part of life."
3. "If at first you don't succeed, try, try again."

Therefore:

1. Assume the best in people.
2. *Tzedakah* brings respect and hope to others.
3. There are many ways to perform *tikkun olam*—just keep doing it.

Now, here I am—a grateful, Jewish American woman with a daughter who teaches the joy of Judaism and the study of Jewish text and who performs acts of kindness daily as well as a granddaughter who knows that we make this a better world by first being respectful and loving to our family. Then, we spread our wings to embrace and include our community.

Dorice Horenstein, Jewish educator

"Give while your hands are still warm." – my mother's words

Abby Levine, director of Jewish Social Justice Roundtable, mother

"How wonderful it is that nobody need wait a single moment before starting to improve the world." – Anne Frank

Lois Wallin Sanchez, life coach

MY MOTHER'S PRIORITY IS AND HAS ALWAYS BEEN KIND-ness to everyone, even if they don't deserve it. She believed no act of kindness, no matter how small, was ever wasted. She extended her kindness into the world by packing delicious sandwiches neatly placed in brown paper bags for people on the streets of Manhattan, many of whom were regarded at that time as "bums" and "drunks." My father had the job of giving those sandwiches out, every day, as he walked to work with Mother's instructions: "Don't touch anyone Al—there could be germs!"

My mother and my father brought food for the hungry, for those commonly regarded as dirty bums who were largely judged and ignored by most passers-by. And, they didn't do it occasionally. They did it not for weeks, not for months, but for years. My parents chose to create ripples of goodness in this world by directly showing others they cared!

Fern Winkler Schlesinger, community leader, educator, philan-thropist, mother

AS JEWS, WE HAVE BEEN BROUGHT UP WITH THE CON-cept of *tikkun olam*. But, repairing the world is more than just doing the right thing or just acting on our concerns. What also matters is how we go about it, which is as important as responding to the need itself. Simply feeling sympathy for another person can be as destructive as it is helpful. If you just take half a step back and empathize with those you wish to help, you will be able to look at what the true need might be and how you can make a lasting difference in another's life. When that occurs, you are able to help others to help themselves. In so doing, you are teaching others to continue the work you have begun by giving back to the community.

For Further Reflection

✳ *Have you extended kindness in the world?*

✳ *In looking forward, how might you extend kindness in the future?*

chapter three

Taking Action

Judith Margles, director of Oregon Jewish Museum and Center for Holocaust Education

IN *HEAVENLY TORAH*, ABRAHAM JOSHUA HESCHEL invokes *midrash* (a form of commentary, sometimes legal, on Biblical text) to support an ethic in which "social responsibility takes precedence over everything." Social responsibility, for Heschel, is a distinctively legal obligation, a *mitzvah*. Judaism mandates positive behavior, a unique innovation in law. You must take action and responsibility for the world—avoiding injustice is not enough.

Jewish women in Portland, Oregon, took this obligation to heart from the moment of their arrival in the Pacific Northwest. These spirited women established chapters of the National Council of Jewish Women and Hadassah along with synagogue sisterhoods and community organizations. Their highest priority was helping others, and so they even put philanthropy above social engagement.

Their oral histories—archived at the Oregon Jewish Museum and Center for Holocaust Education—reveal richly textured portraits of a generation of Jewish women who served as our first community organizers. They built a settlement house for new immigrants to assimilate to American culture, established an orphanage, participated in the women's suffrage movement, and spent countless hours helping those in need. These women have been followed by generations of others, and they inspire me to make the world a better place.

❋

Ruth Messinger, global ambassador for American Jewish World Service

I WORK IN AND OUTSIDE THE JEWISH COMMUNITY TO make social change and create a greater degree of justice in the world. What I have learned from this experience is: "We cannot retreat to the luxury of being overwhelmed."

I know many Jews who are motivated to act for others but not sure how to proceed and also many who are activists working for social change who become discouraged and cut back or stop being involved. They talk about the frustratingly slow pace at which change occurs, how many setbacks arise, how many different issues and challenges there are competing for their attention.

Often, people say that it is too much, that they are overwhelmed, that because they cannot do everything, they cannot do anything. I certainly reassure them we all feel this way some of the time, but to feel or be overwhelmed and use that as an excuse to move away from work for social justice is a convenient out. It is a luxury we simply cannot allow ourselves to enjoy when we know there are human beings in trouble, in need of our not retreating.

It is our responsibility to work through the feeling of being overwhelmed, find ways in which we can make a difference, and remember our tradition teaches that to save one life is to save the world.

For Further Reflection

✳ *In what ways might you pursue the mitzvah of social responsibility?*

✳ *How can we avoid using "the luxury of being overwhelmed" as an excuse?*

Your Wisdom

SECTION FIVE

MOTHERS' WISDOM

chapter one

One-Liners That Teach a Lesson

Marie Abrams, former chair of Jewish Council for Public Affairs

"Even Mary Poppins was only practically perfect."

Linda Abromson, political activist, former mayor of Portland, Maine

I always told my kids, "Don't cry because it is over; laugh because it happened."

Michele Alkin, communications director at Simon Wiesenthal Center

"If it is meant to be (beshert), it will be." – words from my incredibly wise and loving mother

Sheri Cordova, Jewish professional

"A grudge is the heaviest burden you can carry." – my maternal grandmother of blessed memory

"When you open your hand, be sure you have also opened your heart!" – my great-aunt of blessed memory

"Treat your family as friends, and treat your friends as family." – my paternal grandmother of blessed memory

Marlene Dodinval, non-profit professional, mother

ALWAYS LEAVE YOURSELF ROOM TO BE WRONG. THERE is no place for 100 percent certainty—there is always the possibility of new facts and opinions.

Be the bigger person and apologize first. Initiate the healing after a conflict.

"Always eat what is served to you in someone else's home, even if you don't like it. The cook or host has put time and effort into preparing it, and it is rude to refuse it." – my mother

Bev Eastern, community volunteer

My mother always told me, *"Don't brag about your children. Let others do it for you."* And, she was right!

Lindie Henderson, full-time volunteer

LEARN HOW TO SOOTHE YOURSELF SO YOU CAN BE responsive rather than reactive. Separate your needs from your wants and prioritize your search. Consider that the truth is what is real and that honesty is your opinion of what you see, know, or experience.

Abby Levine, director of Jewish Social Justice Roundtable, mother

"In every situation, poor people have it harder than everyone else." – my mother

Sylvia Pearlman, mother, grandmother

WHEN THINGS WEREN'T GOING RIGHT, *"YOU GET USED to hanging if you hang long enough."* – my mother

When friends found mates, and I questioned the match, *"God sits up there, and pairs them up down here."* – my mother

From a friend to her son leaving for camp the first time, *"You've got a mouth—use it."*

One that I use when recommending caution, *"What goes around, comes around."*

Cindy Posen, CPA, community volunteer, mother, grandmother

ALWAYS SAY "I LOVE YOU" WHEN SAYING GOODBYE, AS you never know when you will no longer have the chance to say it again to that person.

Ardyth Shapiro, teacher, singer, gemologist, designer of fine jewelry

THESE WORDS RING IN MY EARS AND MY HEART, AND I live by them:

"There is one God, a loving and forgiving God."

"Live by the Golden Rule."

"The harder you work, the luckier you get."

"Always leave a good taste when you leave someone."

"Don't do anything that will make it so you can't look at yourself in the mirror and like yourself."

"Make a difference in this world because you existed."

"Honesty, responsibility, loyalty, caring for others and family should cover you with a coat of love."

All of these words were said over and over by my parents and became a part of my soul.

Lori Shapiro, rabbi, artistic director

MY GRANDMOTHER ALWAYS TAUGHT MY MOTHER WHO then taught me the rule of three: Always give another the benefit of the doubt. Then, they should give you the benefit of the doubt. After this, there is no doubt.

Lois Shenker, author, teacher, life coach, mother, grandmother

FREQUENTLY SPOKEN THOUGHTS FROM MY MOTHER:

"Live graciously every day."

"We work and work together until the work is done."

"Never show a fool half-finished work."

"Live in such a way that you can look in the mirror every night before you go to bed."

"*Always be nice to everyone. You never know when your past is coming back to you.*"

"*The most important ingredient in a happy marriage is a sense of humor. Don't take yourself too seriously.*"

And the one I still hear in my head on a regular basis: "*Make it easy on yourself, Honey.*"

For Further Reflection

✳ *What are the "one-liners" by which you live?*

chapter two
Words of Wisdom

Marla Feldman, rabbi, executive director of Women of Reform Judaism

"I Shall Not Should on Myself Today." My mother kept these words posted on her refrigerator. I think of them often as I "should" my way through life. I should finish this or that task. I should get more work done. I should take some time off. I should lose weight. I should exercise. I should read that book on my shelf. I should spend more time helping others. I should take more time for myself. Ad infinitum.

"Shoulding" myself leads to impossible standards, mutually exclusive demands on my time, and adds layers of guilt onto my daily life. Who needs that? When I get overwhelmed with all the "shoulds" in my life, I remember Mom's message. I stop "shoulding" myself, and I give myself a break. It feels incredibly liberating!

Marni Fogulson, writer

You get to be the mother you want to be, regardless of how you were mothered. I don't know when I realized this or if someone else told me, but the knowledge that I could create my own mothering traditions and respond to my children in a different way than my mother responded to me (or the very same way) was incredibly liberating. There is no set path for motherhood (either how you get there or what you do when you arrive as a mother). And, best of all, you grow and change as your children do!

Carol Isaak, photographer, art museum docent, rabbi's wife, parent

NEVER A BABYSITTER, UNFAMILIAR WITH BABIES AND young children, it became quite clear to me when I had my own children—they each come into the world with their own personalities. Our job as parents is to support that personality, not interfere with it. Never assume, as did our parents' generation, that a child is a "tabula rasa" (blank slate) onto which we can write whatever we parents choose. What we can do is bring a happy experience of what we value to them. Whether it is religious practice or a taste for art or music, pleasurable exposure is key. Pressure to embrace our own thing is to flirt with disappointment, pain, and possible failure.

Margie Jacobs, rabbi, mother

IN A LETTER TO HER CHILDREN, TO BE READ AFTER HER death, my grandmother wrote: "There comes a time when one has to accept the changes of life that occur with the passing of time. My hope is that you will treasure one another, always, and never forget who and what you are. Material things, over a lifetime, sometimes lose their importance."

Lora Meyer, community volunteer, wife, mother, grandmother

A COLLECTION OF 18 STUNNING CRYSTAL HEARTS IS ONE of my most prized possessions. Each one is different from the others, and the glow of these objects is a constant reminder to me of how each of our hearts beats and sustains our lives.

For most of my life, I have been guided by the examples of

caring, connecting, and compassion which my mother transmitted to me through her commitment to family, Jewish tradition, *tikkun olam*, and *tzedakah*. I have always endeavored to connect family, friends, and strangers in meaningful ways and to recognize the importance of being respectful of each life. Insuring justice and doing righteous deeds are at the heart of my being. Caring hearts are full of love and compassion which enhance our inner selves to fill our world with luminous beauty and significance.

Carol Petrofsky, director of Stanford Wellness and Health Promotion, wellness counselor

"I just visited Sarah in the Alzheimer's home. I can't go back. It's too heart breaking," I sobbed to Karen. Karen, Sarah, and I were best friends, strong accomplished women. Now, Sarah no longer remembers how to talk, how to use a hairbrush, how to move.

My lament flooded me with memories of my Bubbe (grandmother) at our family funerals. The weeping and moans of Mom and my *tantes* (aunts) at gravesites pierced me. But Bubbe sobbed the hardest as she stroked my face, whispering, "Cry, Bubbala. There is nothing so whole as a broken heart."

Bubbe taught me the radical act of surrendering the useless struggle against grief: to gaze into the heart of suffering, to trust our soul to soften, to allow in the light and the small, still courageous voice of love.

Vulnerable and raw, I honor Bubbe. I will, broken-hearted, return soon to visit Sarah. I will love again.

Hannah Rosenthal, president and CEO of Milwaukee Jewish Federation, first woman executive director of a national Jewish organization (JCPA), Special Envoy of Office to Monitor and Combat Anti-Semitism at the US State Department

MY MOTHER, FULL OF WISDOM AND KINDNESS, TOLD ME to always do the right thing. So how do I know what is the right thing? The answer is: When silence would loudly indicate indifference; when the vulnerable people have no voice; when you do something for someone who cannot possibly be of help to you; when the small voice inside you says get over your fear and just act.

My sister, full of humility and generosity, told me to always pursue justice. How do I do so? To be passionate about a cause; to be compassionate towards those you are trying to help; to be tenacious when you feel like you are failing and not making a difference; to recognize the importance of taking even small steps—they all count.

My daughter, full of thoughtfulness and curiosity, asked me what happens after we die. I told her that the only path to immortality is through memory. We are part of a continuum as a family, as a people, as humanity—and that calls for telling stories about each other and saying *kaddish* (memorial prayer).

Beth Reisbard, educator, fund raiser

AS A TEENAGER, MY DAUGHTER WAS ASKED WHAT IT WAS like to have a mother dedicated to the Jewish community. She responded by saying, "We always knew the family came first." The family was primary, but I attempted to instill in my children, grandchildren, and community the importance that we cannot ever be bystanders! Stand up and act for what is right and righteous.

Susan Turnbull, immediate past chair of Jewish Council for Public Affairs, mother, grandmother

WHEN WE WERE MOVING FROM OUR FAMILY HOME OF close to thirty years, I was beside myself. How could I part with my adult sons' prized possessions from their childhood? How could I give away the pink shell that was in my parents' house that I never really liked in the first place? How could we part with files from our first jobs or the warped record albums we had not listened to in decades? I was distraught.

My close friend gave me the best advice. She said, "Take pictures of things you love, and when in doubt, throw it out." So, the thirty-year-old fabric wall-hanging that had been in the basement is now a photo on my phone, and I look at it often.

For Further Reflection

* *What word(s) might you use instead of "should"?*

* *How does the phrase, "You get to be the mother you want to be" translate for you as a mother?*

* *As a daughter?*

* *What are the "words of wisdom" that have guided your life?*

Your Wisdom

CHAPTER THREE

Stories With Meaning

Marie Abrams, former chair of Jewish Council for Public Affairs

I BELIEVE CHILDREN ARE NOT BORN WITH MANNERS OR values, and it is our responsibility to teach them both. If you want your children to become adults who have a good value system and pursue justice, then you must teach them by your actions.

When my children were very young, I had a saying framed on the kitchen wall that said, "The only two lasting bequests you can leave your children are roots and wings." I told any of my friends who noticed it that the roots are much easier than the wings, but equally important. You want your children to become adults who care about their family and their community, who value living an ethical life, and who feel a passion as well as a requirement to repair the world.

So when our adult son told someone who was talking about giving *tzedakah*, that he never knew it was optional—that he just always thought that was what he was supposed to do—I felt somehow I had accomplished a great feat. And, when our daughter decided she not only wanted to become involved in the Jewish community but also began assuming increasingly important leadership roles and told me she was trying to do what she had seen me do—my heart smiled.

Ida Rae Cahana, cantor at Congregation Temple Beth Israel

WHEN I WAS IN MY EARLY TWENTIES, MY MOTHER AND aunt were diagnosed with breast cancer. They went through surgery, treatment, and with the strength and support of loving family and friends, they became two more of the millions of women who survive this disease.

In 2016, I was diagnosed with a stage one breast cancer. I had surgery and went through treatment, walking a path so many of us fear. At first, I wanted to keep this news to myself and close family, but decided it was best to let my congregation know. While I certainly understand the need for privacy and stillness as a piece of the healing process, I learned firsthand that opening up to another can be a needed release.

We align ourselves with a group of people because of our chosen identity. We mark time with holidays and celebrate together. We also endure pain and mourn losses and struggle with what is incomprehensible.

I am now cancer free and grateful to have a community to lean on. I pray for others and for myself to have the strength to know when to ask for help, when to accept acts of kindness with grace, when to say "no, thank you" without guilt.

Sara Charney, former university teacher, vice president of Women of Reform Judaism, mother

MY LATE MOTHER GAVE ME A BOOK OF POETRY THAT WAS presented to her by her mother on the occasion of her twelfth birthday. It is *A Child's Garden of Verses* by Robert Louis Stevenson.

My mother added her own inscription to me from Keats' "Ode on a Grecian Urn": *"Beauty is truth, truth is beauty,— that is all ye know on earth, and all ye need to know."* I try to live by these words every day of my life.

May my mother's and my grandmother's memories be for blessings.

Barbara Donner, author, mother

I HAD EARLY CHILDHOOD TRAUMA AND ENTERED THERAPY in 1962. I had two little girls at the time, and my biggest concern was wanting to be a good parent. One of the words of wisdom from my therapist: "We want to be perfect parents, but the most important thought to remember is that 'The children need to feel and know you care.' And, yes, read the child care books, but most important is the sincere and open care you will give."

Sherri Feuer, full-time volunteer

MY HEART BROKE INTO A MILLION PIECES WHEN OUR son, Aaron, died of suicide at age 20. When he died, I could have let the struggles go—could have refused to answer the intrusive personal questions. But, that would not have been the right thing to do. Instead, I chose to answer the questions honestly; to open the conversation; to be present when others struggled; and, to try to help those dealing with the unimaginable grief. I chose to open the door wider, so others might see a glimmer of light and hope and take a step forward instead of ending their lives. I chose to speak to anyone who would listen. And, I hoped that I could be present for those who had suffered a tragedy, even though the strain and stress of doing so affected me deeply. It was simply the right thing to do: for Aaron, for those suffering with mental illness, for all of us.

Shawn Fields-Meyer, parent, educator, rabbi, teacher

Food is love. And, preparing food for others is active, aspirational, dreamy love. Mother slices and dices, pours and stirs, sifts and sautés. Grandmother stands over the stove, pulls from the oven, sprinkles with sugar, places on the platter. They are ever imagining the moment of delight, the first bite, the sighs and smiles.

Concise and evocative, the Torah tells the same tale. *V'achalta, v'savata, u'verachta*: you will eat; you will be satisfied; you will bless. The one who prepares and serves food sets in motion these holy steps of daily life. Food lovingly placed is eaten; eating brings fullness; fullness stirs gratitude; gratitude speaks of blessing.

Women, of course, are not the exclusive owners of this sacred cycle. But, history has given us a special affinity. Our kitchens are crowded with guests—our mothers, our grandmothers, our foremothers. They are all there, stirring and pouring, slicing and dicing, whispering their recipes into our ears. And someday, we will crowd into the kitchen of our great-great-granddaughter, and we will smile as she serves her food as love, joining the unbroken chain of blessing.

Irene Hecht, retired academic

For many Jews, the standards of *kashrut* (kosher food laws) may be one of the most important practices of their Jewish identity. I have a very different point of view.

As a survivor of a Japanese internment camp in Manila, I had first-hand experience of the trauma of starvation. I know its stages, starting with a fixation on food that ends with a loss of interest in eating—a choice, if indulged, which results in death.

For me the resulting principles are:

1. Do not waste food. To this day, I am physically offended if people pick at their food or leave anything uneaten on their plate. My children grew up well aware of this foible.

2. Food is never to be played with or wasted. I am cognizant that everything which I ingest has given its life, be it a carrot or cow, so I may continue living.

I respect those who live with the rules of *kashrut*, but for me such rules distract. My aim is to eat with reverence, decorum, and gratitude.

For Further Reflection

✳ *What "stories with meaning" do you carry with you?*

✳ *How have they influenced your actions?*

✳ *What are your "stories with meaning" you might share with others?*

SECTION SIX

WELL-KNOWN JEWISH WOMEN SPEAK OUT

Quotes for Inspiration

Hannah Arendt, writer

"Forgiveness is the key to action and freedom."

Roseanne Barr, actress, comedian, writer, television producer, director

"You can always get better. Nobody can stop you from getting better, and nobody can stop you from trying to make something right."

Mayim Bialik, actress, neuroscientist

"Children are great imitators, so give them something great to imitate."

Barbara Boxer, United States senator

"We have the greatest hospitals, doctors, and medical technology in the world. We need to make them accessible to every American."

"More than anything, I think as our country matures, we recognize that women deserve to be treated with respect and dignity."

Sharon Brous, rabbi at IKAR (a Jewish community) in Los Angeles

"Hope is not naïve. Hope may be the greatest single act of defiance against the politics of pessimism and despair."

Anita Diamant, author

"On the day that the intelligence and talents of women are fully honored and employed, the human community and the planet itself will benefit in ways we can only begin to imagine."

Anne Frank, Holocaust victim, author

"It's really a wonder that I haven't dropped all my ideals, because they seem so absurd and impossible to carry out. Yet I keep them, because in spite of everything, I still believe that people are really good at heart."

Betty Friedan, feminist, author

"A good woman is one who loves passionately; has guts, seriousness, and passionate convictions; takes responsibility; and shapes society."

Debbie Friedman, songwriter of Jewish liturgy

"Remember, out of what emerges from life's painful challenges will come our healing."

Ruth Bader Ginsburg, Supreme Court Justice

"I am a judge—born, raised, and proud of being a Jew. The demand for justice runs through the entirety of Jewish tradition. I hope [that] I will have the strength and courage to remain constant in the service of that demand."

Blu Greenberg, feminist as applied to Orthodox Judaism, author

"Where there's a rabbinic will, there's a halakhic [halacha, Jewish law] way."

Goldie Hawn, actress, director, producer

"The lotus is the most beautiful flower whose petals open one by one. But, it will only grow in the mud. In order to grow and gain wisdom, first you must have the mud—the obstacles of life and its suffering. ... The mud speaks of the common ground that humans share, no matter what our stations in life. ... Whether we have it all or we have nothing, we are all faced with the same obstacles: sadness, loss, illness, dying, and death. If we are to strive as human beings to gain more wisdom, more kindness, and more compassion, we must have the intention to grow as a lotus and open each petal one by one."

Erica Jong, author

"I think feminism means what it has always meant—women want to use all their gifts, all their talents and be judged impartially for them. I don't think feminism has ever meant anything else."

Elena Kagan, Supreme Court Justice

"Law matters, because it keeps us safe, because it protects our most fundamental rights and freedoms, and because it is the foundation of our democracy."

Fran Lebowitz, author, public speaker

"The opposite of talking isn't listening. The opposite of talking is waiting."

Deborah Lipstadt, professor of Jewish studies, author

"A creative, thoughtful people such as the Jewish people should be known by what they have done and not by what has been done to them."

Marlee Matlin, actress

"You can do anything if you set your mind to it. … We teach

calculus in schools, but I believe the most important formula is courage plus dreams equals success."

Golda Meir, Prime Minster of Israel

"Trust yourself. Create the kind of self that you will be happy to live with all your life. Make the most of yourself by fanning the tiny, inner sparks of possibility into flames of achievement."

Ruth Messinger, global ambassador for American Jewish World Service

(See page 150)

Cynthia Ozick, short story writer, novelist, essayist

"In saying what is obvious, never choose cunning. Yelling works better."

Dorothy Parker, poet, short story writer, critic, satirist

"The cure for boredom is curiosity. There is no cure for curiosity."

Letty Cottin Pogrebin, editor, writer

"Family conflicts—the trade-offs of your money or your life, your

job or your child—would not be forced upon women with such sanguine disregard if men experienced the same career stalls caused by the-buck-stops-here responsibility for children."

Ayn Rand, novelist, philosopher, playwright, screenwriter

"The evil of the world is made possible by nothing but the sanction you give it."

Kyra Sedgwick, actress

"I think that women as a group are so powerful. I still don't think we are able to embrace our power well enough yet. We think we live in a man's world, and we have to follow their rules, and yet, we're so different, and our rules are so different. I wish that we could come together more as a political force. If women ran the world, I don't believe that there would be war. I really don't. ... We understand the bigger picture. We understand our impact on the environment, on the world. We understand the generations that will go after."

Gloria Steinem, feminist, journalist, political activist

"I have yet to hear a man ask for advice on how to combine marriage and a career."

"Law and justice are not always the same. When they aren't, destroying the law may be the first step toward changing it."

Barbra Streisand, singer, songwriter, actress, filmmaker

"How I wish we lived in a time when laws were not necessary to safeguard us from discrimination."

Diane von Furstenberg, fashion designer

"Generosity is the best investment."

"Attitude is everything."

Barbara Walters, television journalist, interviewer, personality

"Motherhood is tough. If you just want a wonderful little creature to love, you can get a puppy."

"One may walk over the highest mountain one step at a time."

Your Wisdom

Conclusion

Wisdom can be attained from a multitude of places. From the rabbis of long ago to today's wisdom of mothers and voices of women and everything in between, the words that we receive and cherish guide our lives.

From the *Mishnah* in Chapter 6, *Mishnah* 6 of *Pirkei Avot*, we are taught:

"Torah is greater than the priesthood or sovereignty, for sovereignty is acquired with thirty virtues, the priesthood with twenty-four, and Torah is acquired with forty-eight qualities. These are: study, listening, verbalizing, comprehension of the heart, awe, fear, humility, joy, purity, serving the sages, companionship with one's contemporaries, debating with one's students, tranquility, study of the scriptures, study of the Mishnah, minimizing engagement in business, minimizing socialization, minimizing pleasure, minimizing sleep, minimizing talk, minimizing gaiety, slowness to anger, good heartedness, faith in the sages, acceptance of suffering, knowing one's place, satisfaction with one's lot, qualifying one's words, not taking credit for oneself, likableness, love of God, love of humanity, love of charity, love of justice, love of rebuke, fleeing from honor, lack of arrogance in learning, reluctance to hand down rulings, participating in the burden of one's fellow, judging him to the side of merit, correcting him, bringing him to a peaceful resolution [of his disputes], deliberation in study, asking and answering, listening and illuminating, learning in order to teach, learning in order to observe, wising one's teacher, exactness in conveying a teaching, and saying something in the name of its speaker... ."

These words from the writings of our learned ancestors can help move us toward righteous living.

Like *Pirkei Avot*, *Pirkei Imahot* brings essential qualities to our attention, among them are listening to one another, teaching others, supporting others, loving, challenging, apologizing, breathing, believing, and standing up for what is right.

From today's voices of women in the Pirkei Imahot section of this book, we have modern-day wisdom submitted from generous women throughout our country, giving us their own guidelines for daily living. While too numerous to list and too meaningful to select only a few, these lessons are from their own experiences. The women who wrote them have lived these words and learned from them. Each one is a gem, a precious bit of learning to be savored, thought about, acted upon, and hopefully read and re-read over time, providing us with focus, direction, and support. Some are very basic and are lessons or thoughts we will want to share with others or pass on to our children, if we have them. Others will be smiled at as we remember our own mothers and mentors who said or taught us similar things. Still others will cause us to say, "I wish I had said that!"

These comments, so beautifully articulated with warmth and love, contain wisdom of value. They provide a 21st century ethical roadmap from women who have used them in their own lives in the hope that others can learn from them and use them as well. We hope you will take their messages to heart and think about what your own words of wisdom will be as you move forward in your lives.

The sharing of wisdom links us *L'dor V'dor*, from generation to generation, whether it comes from the teachings of long-ago rabbis who were men or from the teachings of contemporary women. This chain of tradition is carried on by our use of their wisdom to participate actively in *tikkun olam,* to help repair the world. This means pursuing justice in every possible way, righting wrongs, helping those in need, and giving of our resources and time when they are needed…in other words, living an ethical life.

May *Pirkei Imahot: The Wisdom of Mothers, The Voices of Women* guide you as you walk your journey.

Visit our website **www.wisdomofmothers.com**

- To purchase books
- For other uses of this book
- For suggested study opportunities
- To participate in and contribute to further projects
- To join the conversation
- For more information

Acknowledgements

riting and editing a book doesn't just happen by itself. There are many people who helped in the process whom we would like to thank, beginning with Congregation Neveh Shalom.

It was our synagogue who brought us together to study. Since our first meeting for that purpose, Congregation Neveh Shalom, its staff, board, and congregants, have been supportive of our work and study together. It is with our appreciation in mind that the major part of the net proceeds from *Pirkei Imahot* will be going to Congregation Neveh Shalom to support programs for youth and education.

We especially want to thank Ruth Messinger for writing the foreword. Even more important than her writing the foreword for us was her endorsement of what we were trying to do. It gave us confidence, encouragement, and an amazing kind of credibility. We are most appreciative.

There are not enough words to thank our editor and friend, Jennifer McGrath, for her outstanding editing, attention to detail, suggestions and ideas, and tireless effort on behalf of us and our book. *Pirkei Imahot* simply would not be what it is without her dedicated efforts. She is an editor *par excellence,* and we were so lucky to have her.

We also want to acknowledge:

Our publisher, Patricia Marshall and her team at Luminare Press;

Rabbi Joshua Stampfer for his early, enthusiastic support of what was then only an idea;

Rabbi Shawn and Tom Fields-Meyer for their expertise and input;

William T. Ayton for designing and publishing our website;

Ken Klein and Bruce Wolf for creating the video on the website;

The many wonderful women who shared their words of wisdom with us and those special women in our lives from whom we have learned and been inspired;

Our children: Shiri and Matan Gilman, Joel and Debbie Shenker, Diana Ayton-Shenker and Bill Ayton, Jordan and Tracey Shenker, and their families, from whom we have learned and continue to learn, who bring us joy and energy to move forward, who inspire us to participate in tikkun olam, and in large part are the reason we do what we do; and

Our husbands, Duncan Gilman and Arden Shenker, without whom none of this could have happened. Their constant encouragement, love, and support is "the wind beneath our wings."

Glossary

The following Hebrew and Yiddish words, which appear in this book, are translated here for your understanding. When they appear in the book, they are in italics and are defined within the text as well. All words are Hebrew unless the word Yiddish appears in the definition.

aveirah transgression

avodah literally means work. Refers to service of the Temple or worship.

avot fathers

Bereshit literally means "in the beginning." It is the first word in the Hebrew Bible and refers to the first Torah portion in the book of Genesis.

b'tzelem Elohim in God's image

Bubby or **Bubbe** Yiddish for grandmother

Hashem literally means "the name" but is used as another name for God

imahot mothers

kaddish literally means holy. Serves as a break between sections of the prayer service. Most commonly refers to the Mourner's Prayer.

kashrut kosher food laws

kedusha holiness

kli, kley (pl) vessel

kodesh holy

kosi revayah my cup is overflowing

l'chaim literally means "to life" and is commonly used as a toast before a glass of wine. It can also mean having a glass of wine, as in "Let's have a l'chaim together."

l'dor v'dor from generation to generation

midrash, midrashim (pl) an ancient commentary on part of the Hebrew scriptures attached to the biblical text. The earliest midrashim come from the 2nd century AD, although much of their content is older.

mensch a Yiddish word that literally means man but is commonly used to refer to one who is an honorable, morally-upright person

Mishnah an authoritative collection of exegetical material embodying the oral tradition of Jewish law and forming the first part of the Talmud. Also, can refer to an individual section of the collection.

mitzvah, mitzvot (pl) literally means commandment, but is commonly used to mean good deed.

neshama soul

shul Yiddish for synagogue

tallit prayer shawl

tantes aunts

tikkun olam repairing the world

tocho k'varo the inside is like the outside

Torah refers to the first five books of the Hebrew Bible in its literal sense. It also refers to the entirety of Jewish learning.

tzedakah literally means righteousness, but commonly used to refer to giving charity.

Yiddish a Jewish language primarily taken from German and added to by the local languages wherever Jews lived.

Yehudim Jews

z"l (zichrono livracha) follows the name of a deceased person and means "may his, or her, memory be for a blessing."

Index of Contributors

About the Authors

Rabbi Eve Posen serves as the Assistant Rabbi at Congregation Neveh Shalom in Portland, Oregon, where she teaches, preaches, inspires, and engages all generations of the synagogue community. Previously, Rabbi Posen spent four years as Campus Rabbi of Ann and Nate Levine Academy in Dallas, Texas. Born and raised in the suburbs of Detroit, Michigan, Rabbi Posen attended the University of Michigan, Ann Arbor, where she received a B.A. in Judaic Studies. She also holds a Master's Degree in Experiential Education from the American Jewish University's Fingerhut School of Education. Upon her ordination from the Ziegler School of Rabbinic Studies at AJU in 2010, she received the SREL (Schechter Residency in Educational Leadership) Fellowship. Rabbi Posen is married to Duncan Gilman, and their children Shiri and Matan are a constant source of inspiration.

LOIS SUSSMAN SHENKER IS A WRITER, TEACHER, AND Life Coach. In addition to her teaching experiences, her career positions include Director of the Early Childhood Learning Center at the Mittleman Jewish Community Center in her hometown of Portland, Oregon, Administrator of the Oregon Board of Rabbis Introduction to Judaism classes, and facilitator/teacher of Mother's Circle, a course on raising Jewish children. Her volunteer service in her community spans decades. She is the author of two previous books: *Welcome to the Family: Opening Doors to the Jewish Experience* and *A Blessed Dying*. Lois and Arden, her husband of 56 years, are the proud parents of three children and their mates, ten grandchildren and four great-grandchildren.